FACE2FACE

21ST CENTURY LESSONS *from* 21 BIBLE HEROES

abraham . barnabas . caleb . daniel
david . elijah . esther . ezekiel
jesus . john the apostle
john the baptist . jonah . joseph
joshua . 3 marys . moses . nehemiah
paul . peter . ruth . timothy

Book 1. Abraham to David

SIMON WARD

Thanks to my former colleagues at the British Fashion Council who, probably unknown to them, supported me through some difficult times in my day to day work, during a period of huge challenge, as I wrote this book. And, particularly, to my daughter Charlotte who, in a ten minute conversation at the height (or depth) of it all, demonstrated a compassion and understanding that still brings a tear to my eye. My wife, Gill is always beside me and I could do none of this without her. Thank you.

Simon Ward
Spring 2019

white bench publishing

www.simonwardlondon.com

Copyright © Simon Ward 2019

All rights reserved. No part of this publication may be reproduced, stored in a retrieval system, or transmitted in any form or by any means, electronic, mechanical, photocopying or otherwise, without the prior written consent of the publisher. Short extracts may be used for review purposes.

Unless othwerwise noted, Scripture quotations from the Holy Bible, New International Version Anglicised, NIV Copyright © 1979, 1984, 2011 by Biblica, Inc. Used by permission. All rights reserved worldwide.

CONTENTS

page

1.	ABRAHAM		**father of the nations**	*1*
		feature	under the microscope	*17*
2.	JESUS	Jesus 1.	a king is born	*29*
3.	BARNABAS		**benefactor & missionary**	*31*
		Jesus 2.	woman at the well	*39*
		Jesus 3.	woman caught in adultery	*39*
4.	CALEB		**team leader**	*41*
		Jesus 4.	widow's mite	*49*
5.	DANIEL		**overseas diplomat**	*51*
		Jesus 5.	calming the storm	*61*
		Jesus 6.	mary & martha	*61*
6.	DAVID		**shepherd, soldier, psalmist, king**	*63*
		Jesus 7.	faith of a canaanite woman	*93*

SINCE WE ARE SURROUNDED BY SUCH A GREAT CLOUD OF WITNESSES, LET US THROW OFF EVERYTHING THAT HINDERS AND THE SIN THAT SO EASILY ENTANGLES AND LET US RUN WITH PERSERVERANCE THE RACE MARKED OUT FOR US *Hebrews 12:1*

INTRODUCTION

MILLENNIA of history may separate us from characters we read about in the Bible, but it doesn't take a PhD in imagination to apply the principles and example of their lives to draw inspiration for our own daily journeys.

This series of four books looks into 21 Old and New Testament lives. It was birthed through the ongoing grappling in my own life between what I see with my eyes and feel in my emotions, and what I understand in my head and believe with all my heart.

Picking my way through the Bible stories, I have intentionally avoided Commentaries, but rather have pondered, through the lens of my own thoughts and experience, what motivated these heroes of old.

And heroes they are, not because they got it all right - that would render them useless for this particular exercise - but precisely because they struggled, as I do, with success and failure, oscillating between satisfying achievement and all too regular frustration.

The longer I have spent with them, the more I have grown in admiration and love for these men and women. There will be plenty to chew over, as we meet in that great and glorious day when we will see, face to face, our Maker, our Redeemer and our forebears in person. For the time being we must look and see them but partially, as in a mirror.

FOR NOW WE SEE ONLY A REFLECTION AS IN A MIRROR; THEN WE SHALL SEE FACE TO FACE. NOW I KNOW IN PART; THEN I SHALL KNOW FULLY, EVEN AS I AM FULLY KNOWN
1 Corinthians 13:12

Simon Ward
2013

Author's Note: this book never saw the light of day when it was first written, for a number of reasons. As it still seems relevant, I am now allowing it to emerge, blinking, into the daylight of 2019, although I have moved on in some areas: eg retiring from full-time work in 2016. I survived - Yay! SW

1 ABRAHAM
father of the nations

ABRAHAM

DESCENDANTS AS COUNTLESS AS THE SAND ON THE SEASHORE
Genesis 22:17

RIGHTEOUS MAN OF FAITH

By faith Abraham, when called to go to a place he would later receive as his inheritance, obeyed and went, even though he did not know where he was going. By faith he made his home in the promised land like a stranger in a foreign country; he lived in tents, as did Isaac and Jacob, who were heirs with him of the same promise. For he was looking forward to the city with foundations, whose architect and builder is God.

And by faith even Sarah, who was past childbearing age, was enabled to bear children because she considered him faithful who had made the promise.

And so from this one man, and he as good as dead, came descendants as numerous as the stars in the sky and as countless as the sand on the seashore.
Hebrews 11:8-12

MAYBE the best place to start a consideration of Abraham's life is at the end ... as the writer of Hebrews walks us through his Faith Hall of Fame. *(see panel to left)*

From the outset, we see that faith, the great theme of Abraham's life, is not simply a matter of the intellect. It is measured by obedience and action. But the seeming paradox is that it is faith that God looks for, not what we do: *Abram believed the Lord, and he credited it to him as righteousness. (Genesis 15:6)*

Righteousness, being right with God, is not about doing good all the time. That's just as well, as we'll see that Abram [he will become Abraham] got up to some pretty daft stuff! Rather, it is believing God's promises to us and behaving in response to them. This may sound like a New Testament discussion between the apostles Paul and James, but Abram had been there millennia beforehand.

Let's return to the beginning. Abram's dad was Terah. They lived about the same period BC as we are AD. He had brothers, Nahor and Haran, and his wife was Sarai. We are told she was unable to conceive. They set out from Ur of the Chaldeans, close to modern Baghdad, to go to Canaan (modern Israel with a bit of Palestine, Jordan and Syria thrown in). But when they came to Harran (in Turkey) they chose to settle there.

Q. WHAT DOES 'FAITH' MEAN TO ME? AND WHAT DIFFERENCE DOES IT MAKE TO THE WAY I RUN MY LIFE?

Father God, I want an apply to my life the principles adopted by your people of old. Help me as I grapple with the cultural differences to see how I can put into practice the way they did things. Amen.

A GREAT NATION

ABRAHAM

The Lord had said to Abram, "Go from your country, your people and your father's household to the land I will show you. "I will make you into a great nation, and I will bless you; I will make your name great, and you will be a blessing. I will bless those who bless you, and whoever curses you I will curse; and all peoples on earth will be blessed through you." So Abram went, as the Lord had told him; and Lot went with him. Abram was seventy five years old when he set out from Harran. Genesis 12:1-4

I HAD always thought of Abram coming from a nomadic background. Wrong. He grew up in a major cultural city, Ur, and then spent his adult life in Harran, another large urban centre. So, at the age of 75, to be called by God (who presumably didn't present him with a Sat Nav and Top 10 Guide to where he was going) to travel into an unknown land where he would live in tents, was no small ask. There is no indication as to whether Abram responded immediately or went away to weigh up what was being asked of him. We are told, quite simply: *"So Abram went, as the Lord had told him."*

I often find myself pondering this "was called ... and went" scenario that recurs in the Bible. It is not something I have encountered so clearly in my own experience, and I admire those who step out into the unknown from all they are familiar with. To do so, particularly if you are that bit older and more established, must demonstrate either an alarming disregard for your responsibilities, or a very clear judgement that it's God on the line and to "go" is a matter of simple obedience.

Whilst Abram might have had to go to an unknown place, he did not, as we shall shortly see, have to leave behind his worldly goods. And there is a big carrot held in front of Abram - he will become a great nation and be blessed ... and be a blessing to others.

Q. HOW CAN I BE SURE THAT IT IS GOD'S VOICE I AM HEARING WHEN I PRAY?

Father God, I am in awe of Abraham's certainty that You had called him to step out into an unknown world. Reveal to me Your call on my life and grant me the confidence that it is Your voice, and the obedience to act on it - regardless of the magnitude of what is at stake. Amen

I WILL MAKE YOUR NAME GREAT AND YOU WILL BE A BLESSING
Genesis 12:2

TO A NEW LAND

3

Q. DO I INVOLVE THOSE AROUND ME - MY FAMILY, FRIENDS, CHURCH - IN MY DISCERN-MENT OF GOD'S CALL ON MY LIFE?

Father God, help me to know that you call us to relationship before you call us to service. Protect me from taking a 'lone ranger' approach to following you, and open my eyes to see the importance of working plans out together with those I love ... including across the different generations. Amen

THE key to hearing God aright must lie in having an established and close relationship with Him where you get to know His voice in the smaller things, so you are ready for the bigger and more testing challenges. Easy to say (or write); not so easy to do in practice. Clearly Abram decided this was for him and I imagine he must have set off with a mixture of excitement and anxiety:

He took his wife Sarai, his nephew Lot, all the possessions they had accumulated and the people they had acquired in Harran, and they set out for the land of Canaan, and they arrived there. Genesis 12:5

The little phase *"and they arrived there"* is intriguing. It may just be a turn of phrase; or it may refer back to when Abram with his family had originally set out from Ur a few decades earlier. Then, they had been headed for Canaan, but only made it as far as Harran. Had God led Abram's father to move to the Promised Land, but it was his son who would eventually complete the journey?

Like David who conquered the land, but Solomon who built the temple, this is an example of how God works through the generations of families. In an age when independence and personal achievement are so lauded, do we need to recognise that God may see things rather differently ... and thence we must spend more time and effort nurturing the next generation if we want to see God working His purposes out.

THEY SET OUT FOR THE LAND OF CANAAN
Genesis 12:5

... GOD WORKS THROUGH THE GENERATIONS OF FAMILIES. IN AN AGE WHEN INDEPENDENCE AND PERSONAL ACHIEVEMENT ARE SO LAUDED ...

A PLACE TO WORSHIP

ABRAHAM

4

HAVING arrived in Canaan, where we later learn there was a resident culture of idol worship and child sacrifice, Abram set about building altars to worship God:

The Lord appeared to Abram and said, "To your offspring I will give this land." So he built an altar there to the Lord, who had appeared to him. From there he went on toward the hills east of Bethel and pitched his tent, with Bethel on the west and Ai on the east. There he built an altar to the Lord and called on the name of the Lord. Genesis 12:7-8

Q. HOW DO I EXPERIENCE GOD'S PRESENCE?

"The Lord appeared to Abram" raises a simple question in my mind. How?! Did Abram see God face to face? If so, what did He look like? Was it Jesus; or an angel speaking on behalf of God? Or did Abram have a vision during his sleep? One thing is for sure - on both occasions here, he built an altar and worshipped God.

Then Abram "called on the name of the Lord". I take this as offering worship to God. I wonder how Abram and his family worshipped. Would they have thrown back their heads and given a rousing rendition of Jerusalem or Cwm Rhondda (their equivalent, of course)? Or would they have chanted words? Would they have stood or kneeled as they praised Him and gave Him thanks? One thing we can assume is that there was no comfy building with band plugged in to lead the worship (or hard wooden pews with organ). Abram looked around and used what was available to worship God.

Father God, grow in me the creativity to see different ways of worshipping You, regardless of where I am, so that I might develop the habit of rejoicing in You at all times, and in all places, whatever the circumstances. Amen

We too can look around wherever we are and use what is to hand as an aid to worship. It could be praying for those sitting in the train seat opposite; thanking God for the bright morning sunshine; asking God to give peace and strength to the young mum struggling with a pram and howling kids at the supermarket check out; praising God for a news item that shows good overcoming evil; singing praises at the top of your voice like Julie Andrews in the Sound of Music as you walk a favourite path (be careful of others' reaction if you try this). Whatever. Just do it.

REJOICE IN THE LORD ALWAYS. I WILL SAY IT AGAIN: REJOICE!
Philippians 4:4

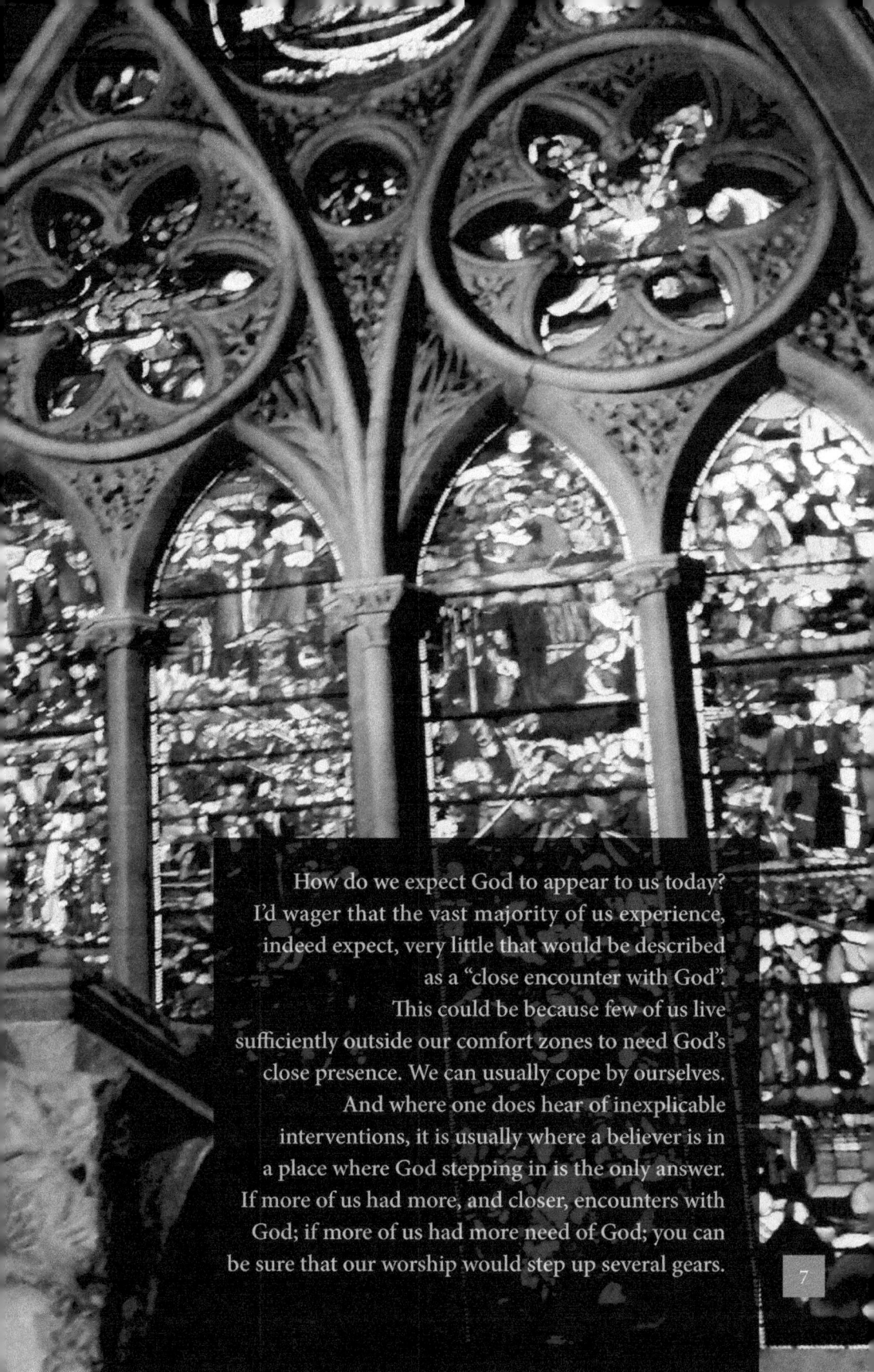

How do we expect God to appear to us today? I'd wager that the vast majority of us experience, indeed expect, very little that would be described as a "close encounter with God". This could be because few of us live sufficiently outside our comfort zones to need God's close presence. We can usually cope by ourselves. And where one does hear of inexplicable interventions, it is usually where a believer is in a place where God stepping in is the only answer. If more of us had more, and closer, encounters with God; if more of us had more need of God; you can be sure that our worship would step up several gears.

MIXED RESPONSE

ABRAHAM

Now there was a famine in the land, and Abram went down to Egypt to live there for a while because the famine was severe. As he was about to enter Egypt, he said to his wife Sarai, "I know what a beautiful woman you are. When the Egyptians see you, they will say, 'This is his wife.' Then they will kill me but will let you live. Say you are my sister, so that I will be treated well for your sake and my life will be spared because of you." Genesis 12:10-13

Q. WHAT IS MY IMMEDIATE RESPONSE TO A CHALLENGING SITUATION?

ABRAM faced two situations here - both unpromising - the prospect of starvation and the possibility of losing his wife and maybe his life. Abram allowed fear to dominate his response to both. Did he get either right?

On the surface, moving on to a land where there was food during a famine was a good call, as he looked to care for those who looked to him. Did he enquire of God, though, before making the move? Had he stayed, might God have provided, as He did years later with manna and quail? What happened to those permanently resident in Canaan - did they stay and survive, or flee? We're not told. It seems, though that this was a good response to an understandable concern.

How about pretending his wife was his sister? (ironic that so much time is spent trying to look beautiful!) Both the reason and the result demonstrate that this was not a good call. Abram was clearly as worried about his own skin as his wife's safety. Not overly heroic!

I wonder what Sarai made of this charade? Particularly when Pharaoh, not unexpectedly, took a shine to her and "took her into his palace" as his own wife, thus committing unwitting adultery ... whilst Abraham was living the high life with livestock, servants and transport laid on.

Father God, Your word says that 'perfect love casts out fear', and yet so often fear is the driver of my reaction when I find myself in a difficult situation. Help me to develop such a close relationship with you that I might immediately turn to You before allowing fear to take the upper hand. Guide me at all times to take decisons that place my trust in You. Amen

SAY YOU ARE MY SISTER SO I WILL BE TREATED WELL
Genesis 12:13

TWO SORTS OF FEAR

6

Q. HAVE I TAKEN BAD DECISONS THAT HAVE LED OTHERS INTO A DIFFICULT PLACE?

Father God, keep me alert at all times to see the effect on others of decisions I take. Grant me the courage to 'love my neighbour' and be truthful, even when that might make life uncomfortable for me - that Your name might be glorified in my integrity. Amen

ABRAM'S ruse that Sarai was his sister - rebounded ... with interest:

But the Lord inflicted serious diseases on Pharaoh and his household because of Abram's wife Sarai. So Pharaoh summoned Abram. "What have you done to me?" he said. "Why didn't you tell me she was your wife? Genesis 12:17-18

Good question! and things could have turned well nasty but, fortunately, Pharaoh took the either conciliatory or fearful view to send them on their way asap.

Why did you say, 'She is my sister,' so that I took her to be my wife? Now then, here is your wife. Take her and go!" Then Pharaoh gave orders about Abram to his men, and they sent him on his way, with his wife and everything he had. Genesis 12:19-20

What happened in Egypt shows that there is the danger of taking a wrong decision on the back of a right decision, where understandable fear surrounds both situations. Having called on the Lord earlier, did Abram forget to discuss these things with God? We all do it, of course, so there's no place here for self righteous tut-tutting.

There are two sorts of fear: fear of the Lord; and fear of situations and people. We need to aim to live by the right one. No prizes for which is which.

The Lord confides in those who fear him; he makes his covenant known to them. Psalm 25:14

Fear and trembling have beset me; horror has overwhelmed me. I said, "Oh, that I had the wings of a dove! I would fly away and be at rest. Psalm 55:5-6

"NEVER MAKE LIFE CHOICES BASED ON FEAR"
    ... the wise words of a work colleague
        ... it's a shame that Abram wasn't listening in

PARTING OF THE WAYS

ABRAHAM

7

ABRAM, his family and entourage, return to Canaan considerably more numerous and wealthy than when they left for Egypt. God blessed them, in spite of Abram's near calamitous deception. This is the sort of God we are dealing with: *"... gracious and compassionate, slow to anger and rich in love." (Psalm 145:8)* ... who *"is the same yesterday and today and forever." (Hebrews 13:8)*

So we, today, can rejoice in a God who will not hold our mistakes against us: *If we confess our sins, he is faithful and just and will forgive us our sins and purify us from all unrighteousness. (1 John 1:9)* That's good news.

But Abram's prosperity brought challenges. Between them, he and his nephew Lot had so much livestock that the land could not support them living together.

So Abram said to Lot, "Let's not have any quarrelling between you and me, or between your herders and mine, for we are close relatives. Is not the whole land before you? Let's part company. If you go to the left, I'll go to the right; if you go to the right, I'll go to the left." Lot looked around and saw that the whole plain of the Jordan toward Zoar was well watered, like the garden of the Lord, like the land of Egypt. (This was before the Lord destroyed Sodom and Gomorrah.) So Lot chose for himself the whole plain of the Jordan and set out toward the east. The two men parted company: Abram lived in the land of Canaan, while Lot lived among the cities of the plain and pitched his tents near Sodom. Now the people of Sodom were wicked and were sinning greatly against the Lord. Genesis 13:8-13

Something fairly obvious jumps off the page here.

Just "looking around", as Lot did, is not adequate when taking a significant decision. Some basic research would have revealed that, whist the plain of the Jordan was well watered, it was populated by people doing bad stuff. Lot pitching his tents there, was an accident waiting to happen. So it will be with us if we simply go by first impressions.

Q. DO I REGULARLY TAKE STOCK OF HOW GOD HAS BLESSED MY LIFE?

Father God, I want to take You seriously in my life. Help me to see the opportunities before me as You see them and guide me to weigh up which are wise options to pursue and which are likely to lead to problems and heartache. Amen

DECISION TAKING

8

MY instinct is to be "light touch" in decision taking. I won't spend weeks looking for just the right shirt, I'll buy one I see and like. If I'm booking somewhere to stay for a weekend away, I'll have a look though some options, but the deal will be done quickly. If I get things like these wrong, it's not the end of the world.

Yet if I take that approach to recruiting staff in the workplace or buying a home, the ramifications, if I don't do adequate homework, are far more difficult and costly (time, energy and relationship, as well as money) to put right.

As I write, I'm having to decide how best to proceed with a recently recruited team member who, it appears, has some issues which we failed to pick up at selection. We've had a number of not dissimilar issues over the last year or two, and I have to look at myself in the mirror and ask: "has my level of due diligence been adequate"? This is basic, sensible procedure.

But, there is also the question of spiritual discernment. Lot didn't just find himself in a place where he needed rescuing from warring local kings, he found that he had chosen to live in a place "where the people ... were wicked and sinned greatly against the Lord". Abram and his men were able to bale Lot out of his physical predicament:

> When Abram heard that his relative had been taken captive, he called out the 318 trained men born in his household and went in pursuit as far as Dan. During the night Abram divided his men to attack them and he routed them, pursuing them as far as Hobah, north of Damascus. He recovered all the goods and brought back his relative Lot and his possessions, together with the women and the other people. Genesis 14:14-16

Q. HOW MUCH DO I INVOLVE GOD IN MY DECISION TAKING?

Father God, grant me wisdom to sense which decisions in my life need specific discernment and Your touch, that I might proceed with confidence that I have carried out 'due diligence' as a representative of Your Kingdom. Amen

HAS MY LEVEL OF DUE DILIGENCE BEEN ADEQUATE?

ABRAHAM

HE WAS PRIEST OF GOD MOST HIGH
Genesis 14:18

MELCHIZEDEK

9

Q. DO I DISCERN 'GOD ENCOUNTERS' WHEN THEY OCCUR IN MY LIFE?

Father God, may I be a blessing to those around me; through the encouraging things I say, the faults I choose to overlook, and the person I am, always available to pray for people and help them out. Amen

BIBLE MYSTERIES NEED TO BE GRAPPLED WITH FOR ... THEY GIVE US INSIGHT INTO THE "OTHERNESS" OF GOD

HAVING rescued Lot, the king of Sodom came out to offer his thanks to Abram for rescuing his people along with Lot and his family. And now one of the Bible's great mystery characters appears:

Then Melchizedek king of Salem brought out bread and wine. He was priest of God Most High, and he blessed Abram, saying, "Blessed be Abram by God Most High, Creator of heaven and earth. And praise be to God Most High, who delivered your enemies into your hand." Then Abram gave him a tenth of everything. Genesis 14:18-20

We could maybe overlook Melchizedek as one of those impossible to pronounce Old Testament characters we hope don't appear in a bible passage we're called on to read out loud. Except he is referred to by David as a model for the future Christ; *"You are a priest forever, in the order of Melchizedek."* Psalm 110:4

And he is then given serious air time in Hebrews, as the writer seeks to explain the priestly role of Jesus by comparing Him with Melchizedek:

This Melchizedek was king of Salem and priest of God Most High. He met Abraham returning from the defeat of the kings and blessed him, and Abraham gave him a tenth of everything. First, the name Melchizedek means "king of righteousness"; then also, "king of Salem" means "king of peace." Without father or mother, without genealogy, without beginning of days or end of life, resembling the Son of God, he remains a priest forever. Hebrews 7:1-3

Bible mysteries need to be grappled with for, even though we often will not come up with a complete or even satisfactory understanding, they give us insight into the "otherness" of God and show us that, for all our wisdom, there is much that we simply cannot grasp.

MYSTERY MAN — ABRAHAM

10

GRAPPLING with mystery will develop in us a humility that will be both a good corrective and a stimulus to pressing closer into God, to know more of Him and His ways. As the writer of Hebrews says when starting to discuss Melchizedek: *We have much to say about this, but it is hard to make it clear to you because you no longer try to understand. Hebrews 5:11*

So, let's have a go at understanding Melchizedek. It's not actually that difficult, as the hard work is done for us by the writer of the book of Hebrews. Scripture often interprets Scripture for us. Melchizedek is presented as anticipating Jesus 2000 years earlier.

There are several parallels: Unlike other significant characters in the Old Testament, no details of either his coming or going are given: *Without father or mother, without genealogy, without beginning of days or end of life, resembling the Son of God, he remains a priest forever. Hebrews 7:3*

This suggestion of endlessness prefigured Christ's eternal nature. But he was not an early appearance by Jesus on earth. *"You (Jesus) are a priest forever, in the order of Melchizedek." Psalm 110:4* His name is linked to titles given to Jesus: *The name Melchizedek means "king of righteousness"; then also, "king of Salem" means "king of peace". Hebrews 7:2*

We are told he is both priest and king, usually separate roles, again foreshadowing Christ's role as King of kings and High Priest. *This Melchizedek was king of Salem and priest of God Most High. Hebrews 7:1*

He blessed Abraham and received a tithe offering from him - making him greater than the Patriarch himself. *Just think how great he was: Even the patriarch Abraham gave him a tenth of the plunder! And without doubt the lesser is blessed by the greater. Hebrews 7:4,7*

SO WHAT? 2 KEY THINGS,
1. The Bible yields great richness and understanding to those who spend time in it.
2. Although we will not fully see it until He returns in glory, Jesus runs like a thread through the whole of human history, if only we would open our eyes of faith to perceive it. Without faith, we'll see only the everyday that passes by before us.

Q. HOW PERSISTENT HAVE I BEEN EXPLORING SCRIPTURE TO BETTER UNDERSTAND THE THINGS OF GOD AND THE PEOPLE HE HAS WORKED THROUGH DOWN THE CENTURIES?

Father God, open my eyes to see the broad sweep of Your story as it's unfolded through the pages of history - the history of the nations, of the church and of my own family - that I might give You the glory for your faithfulness. Amen

ABRAM BELIEVED GOD

11

THE word of the Lord then appears to Abram in a vision as God renews his promise that his offspring will be more numerous than the stars above his head. *Abram believed the Lord, and he credited it to him as righteousness. Genesis 15:6*

God also renews his promise of giving to Abram the land on which he stands. He asks God how he'll know this is true. God tells him to cut up some animals as an offering, lay them in 2 rows and wait to see what happens. Abram does as he's told.

As the sun was setting, Abram fell into a deep sleep, and a thick and dreadful darkness came over him. Then the Lord said to him, "Know for certain that for four hundred years your descendants will be strangers in a country not their own and that they will be enslaved and mistreated there.

But I will punish the nation they serve as slaves, and afterward they will come out with great possessions. You, however, will go to your ancestors in peace and be buried at a good old age. In the fourth generation your descendants will come back here, for the sin of the Amorites has not yet reached its full measure." When the sun had set and darkness had fallen, a smoking fire pot with a blazing torch appeared and passed between the pieces. Genesis 15:12-17

Q. DO I HAVE A GRASP OF THE PROMISES OF GOD AND HOW THEY APPLY TO MY LIFE?

Father God, bring alive the faith You have planted in me, that it might be alive and active, and not simply mental assent to a theoretical propostition. Amen

This mysterious ceremony is based on a traditional ancient format, where the perpetrator is effectively saying "chop me up like this if my word is shown to be untrue". The blazing torch represents God's presence sealing the covenant. So this is heavy stuff - God is explaining 400 years of Israel's history before it happens and saying "on my life be it".

As an aside, I wonder if Abraham's belief here was a silent, mental/emotional acceptance, or an intentional and vocalised "Yes, Lord". Probably the latter, and maybe we need to focus our thought life about God into spoken words, even if we're in the middle of a field or on a busy pavement. This way we can capture for real what might otherwise be passing fancy - and this act of taking God seriously is counted by Him as righteousness.

"LOOK UP AT THE SKY AND COUNT THE STARS IF INDEED YOU CAN COUNT THEM." GOD SAID TO ABRAM, "SO SHALL YOUR OFFSPRING BE" *Genesis 15:5*

UNDER THE MICROSCOPE

THIS thought comes in the middle of writing about Abraham (he's actually the 11th to come under the microscope - the Heroes were not written in order!)

For I've not found the going easy. As is my way, I pause to ponder why this is. It's not that I'm running out of steam - it's great fun delving into the lives of all these wonderful characters.

No, I think it comes down to the relationship between me and the hero under the microscope. For it's me who's also under the microscope, as I try to get under their skin. As I study them, I study myself. And where I find a kindred spirit, the going is relatively straight forward as I understand them, even though I may not always like all that I find out about myself.

But it's harder work with Abraham, as I seem to have precious little in common with him. So I'm struggling to identify what's going on in his life and why. The temptation is to set him aside and move on to someone else who rings my bell. And this would, of course, be the wrong call. For if I'm only interested in people like me, I'm not going to be of much use to the majority of the population ... who are not like me.

I guess it comes down to what James calls The Royal Law: *"Love your neighbour as yourself"* (*James 2:8*)

If I don't try to understand my neighbour, how am I ever going to be in a position to love them. It's an uphill part of the journey. But, when I reach the top, I'm anticipating that the wider view will be more than worth the extra effort.

So, it's time to step out. Onwards and upwards.

Sidebar:

THE RELATIONSHIP BETWEEN ME AND THE HERO UNDER THE MICROSCOPE

AS I STUDY THEM I STUDY MYSELF

I'M STRUGGLING TO IDENTIFY WHAT'S GOING ON IN ABRAHAM'S LIFE AND WHY

IF I DON'T TRY TO UNDERSTAND MY NEIGHBOUR, HOW AM I EVER GOING TO BE IN A POSITION TO LOVE THEM

FALSE UNDERSTANDING

ABRAHAM

AFTER this awesome canvas, what Abram does next seems extraordinarily crass: *Now Sarai, Abram's wife, had borne him no children. But she had an Egyptian slave named Hagar; so she said to Abram, "The Lord has kept me from having children. Go, sleep with my slave; perhaps I can build a family through her." Abram agreed to what Sarai said. Genesis 16:1-2*

There is, of course, a simple logic to what happened. God had said to Abram: "a son who is your own flesh and blood will be your heir". Sarai couldn't bear children, so how else would the promise come about? And, in those days, it appears to have been all the rage to have had a bevy of wives and concubines. So maybe Abraham's actions are understandable. But they were not what God had planned as the resultant pain and discord demonstrate.

Abram slept with Hagar, and she conceived. When she knew she was pregnant, she began to despise her mistress.

Then Sarai said to Abram: "You are responsible for the wrong I am suffering. I put my slave in your arms, and now that she knows she is pregnant, she despises me. May the Lord judge between you and me." Genesis 16:4-5

Sarai, having suggested the ruse in the first place, mistreats Hagar and drives her away. But the words of the angel who comforted Hagar as she fled, echoed those of God to Abram; *"I will increase your descendants so much that they will be too numerous to count." Genesis 16:10*

And so it was to be. The son that was born to Hagar, Ishmael, would be the father of the Arab people who, to this day, have been in conflict with the Jewish people who would be the descendants of Abram's son to come by Sarai. What we do today, and how we do it, have repercussions that run for generations. All the more reason to stay in close touch with God, not just on the destination of our journeying, but how we're going to get there.

The signpost at Lands End shows the direction to John O'Groats and the distance, but not how to travel. We need to work that out separately if we're going to embark on the journey. No use attempting it by pogo stick, we'd never get there. Similarly, it wouldn't be wise to try to cycle the other way ... to New York! Problems would quickly surface! Can you see the comparison with Abram and Hagar?!

Q. DO I TRY AND SECOND GUESS WHAT GOD MIGHT BE DOING IN MY LIFE AND TRY TO MAKE IT HAPPEN AS I SEE IT?

Father God, forgive me where I try to take control of the events in my life - then become downcast or angry when things don't work out. Give me patience to wait for Your perfect timing. Amen

A SIGN OF BELONGING

13

No longer will you be called Abram; your name will be Abraham, for I have made you a father of many nations.
Genesis 17:5

This is my covenant with you and your descendants after you, the covenant you are to keep: Every male among you shall be circumcised. ... Abraham was 99 years old when he was circumcised, and his son Ishmael was 13; Abraham and his son Ishmael were both circumcised on that very day.
Genesis 17:10, 24-26

God also said to Abraham, "As for Sarai your wife, you are no longer to call her Sarai; her name will be Sarah. I will bless her and will surely give you a son by her. I will bless her so that she will be the mother of nations; kings of peoples will come from her."
Genesis 17: 15,16

A LOT goes on in Genesis 17. Abram and Sarai both get name changes: Abraham, meaning father of many. Sarah will give birth to a son to be called Isaac. Ishmael will multiply and be blessed, but God's covenant is with the line though Isaac. And male circumcision is to be the sign of membership of those chosen by God to be His covenant people.

3 POINTS OF INTEREST HERE:

1. Abraham and Sarah's name change coincided with God announcing a covenant with the people that would be their descendants. When we become a Christian, we are born again (John 3:3) and become a new creation (2 Cor 5:17). We don't just join a social club; we become a new person. If we don't understand that, we'll be trapped between a new ideal and old ways we can't throw off.

We will find ourselves in a dilemma similar to that described by the apostle Paul: *So I find this law at work: Although I want to do good, evil is right there with me. What a wretched man I am! Who will rescue me from this body that is subject to death?* **But Paul is clear about the** answer to his own question: *Thanks be to God, who delivers me through Jesus Christ our Lord! (Romans 7:21, 24-25)*
We need to learn how this works out in practice.

2. Isaac appeared very late in the day. From the time God first revealed to Abraham that he would become a great nation, to the birth of Isaac was a quarter of a century. Why the long delay? Was it to show, beyond doubt, that Isaac's birth was of His doing, not his parents? Was the birth of Ishmael and the nations that would descend from him a part of God's plan which would not have come to pass until Abraham was desperate?   ... continued ...

Q. HAVE I GRASPED THAT I AM A NEW PERSON IN CHRIST?

Father God, do a work of transformation in me, to enable me to fully realise that everything is new when I accept Jesus into my life. Amen

LIGHT TO THE NATIONS

... continued ... OR was there some other reason in God's economy that we are not able to see? One thing's for sure - often God takes a lot longer than we want or understand to bring His plans to pass. His timing is not ours. As the apostle Peter observed: *With the Lord a day is like a thousand years, and a thousand years are like a day. (2 Peter 3:8)*

We need to recognise and accept this, or we will experience much frustration in our Christian walk.

3. Israel was God's covenant people chosen, not to live a privileged existence, rather to show His love, character and goodness to the world. To be a light to the nations. It's easy to look back at the Jewish people in the Old Testament and tut tut that they became the largely inward looking people Jesus encountered.

Yet Christians today need to remember that the church exists for the benefit of its non members. Our calling is not to have a nice chummy time together (although there, is of course, much encouragement and support to be shared as the body of Christ). Rather, as Jesus announced to His disciples before ascending to heaven: *Go and make disciples of all nations, baptising them in the name of the Father and of the Son and of the Holy Spirit, and teaching them to obey everything I have commanded you. And surely I am with you always, to the very end of the age." Matthew 28:19-20*

And I reckon there's a wee sting in the tail of that admonition. It will only be when we are actively engaged in His commission that we will know Jesus' close presence with us. The "inactive Christian" will experience little of the richness and empowering of the Holy Spirit, simply because they don't need it. When we step out of our comfort zone in Jesus' name, He will be there beside us.

NB. FOR POTENTIAL WORRIERS - this is not to suggest that, if we're not on the evangelism trail, our eternal destiny becomes unsure. We are saved by faith, accepting God's grace, and not by our own actions.

ABRAHAM

And Abraham said to God, "If only Ishmael might live under your blessing!" Then God said, "Yes, but your wife Sarah will bear you a son, and you will call him Isaac. I will establish my covenant with him as an everlasting covenant for his descendants after him. And as for Ishmael, I have heard you: I will surely bless him; I will make him fruitful and will greatly increase his numbers. He will be the father of twelve rulers, and I will make him into a great nation. But my covenant I will establish with Isaac, whom Sarah will bear to you by this time next year." Genesis 17:15-16, 18-21

Q. DO I CONSIDER MY FAITH TO BE A BADGE OF PRIVILEGE OR A COMMISSION TO REACH OUT THOSE AROUND ME?

Father God, stir up in me a desire to share the transforming love of Jesus with those around me, that it might be a joy rather than a burden. Amen

RECONNAISSANCE DAY TRIP

Q. CAN I SEE JESUS IN THE PEOPLE AROUND ME?

Father God, grant me insight to see something of what You are doing in the everyday situations going on around me. Enable me to discern You at work in the smallest acts of kindness or Your invitation to step in to meet a need, knowing that it is You I am serving. Amen

WHAT comes next, is intriguing: *The Lord appeared to Abraham near the great trees of Mamre while he was sitting at the entrance to his tent in the heat of the day. Abraham looked up and saw three men standing nearby. When he saw them, he hurried from the entrance of his tent to meet them and bowed low to the ground.* Genesis 18:1-2

The story is that the three men are given warm and generous hospitality by Abraham; they announce that Sarah will give birth a year later; they say that they are checking out the sinfulness of Sodom and Gomorrah before destroying them (no need to dwell on the outcome); and Abraham bargains hard that the towns be spared, if anyone righteous (his nephew Lot and family) is found in them (clearly they were the only ones)

Not the stuff of everyday conversation with strangers, but what intrigues me is the "oneness" (they) yet individuality (one of them) of the three men. *"Where is your wife Sarah?" they asked him. .... Then one of them said, "I will surely return to you about this time next year, and Sarah your wife will have a son."* Genesis 18:9-10

They are referred to interchangeably and without explanation. Do we assume that this was the Holy Trinity in human likeness on a reconnaissance day trip? Or were they angels, as is implied by the writer of Hebrews: *Do not forget to show hospitality to strangers, for by so doing some people have shown hospitality to angels without knowing it.* Hebrews 13:2

And we are told, in the midst of it, that the voice of the Lord spoke: *Then the Lord said, "The outcry against Sodom and Gomorrah is so great and their sin so grievous that I will go down and see if what they have done is as bad as the outcry that has reached me. If not, I will know."* Genesis 18:20-21

ABRAHAM LOOKED UP AND SAW
THREE MEN STANDING NEARBY

MULTI MEDIA LISTENING

ABRAHAM

16

NO wonder we can get confused at how God speaks to us. And haven't we all heard comments along the lines of "God told me to do this" or "The Lord said that." What is His voice and what isn't? That God speaks ... to us ... today ... cannot be in doubt:

For the word of God is alive and active. Sharper than any double-edged sword, it penetrates even to dividing soul and spirit, joints and marrow; it judges the thoughts and attitudes of the heart. Hebrews 4:12

For me, I find myself challenged and moved through a variety of media, including: spending time with God's Word (obviously); looking around me at God's handiwork (nature) and man's handiwork (buildings, gardens, organisations, relationships); and, in recent years, by grappling with what I find and have experienced through photography and writing (what you are reading!).

One key means of listening out for God is to listen to what people say to me. And often people who, to my knowledge, have very little to do with God, can come out with words showing truly Godly insight, that challenge my faith and my daily walk.

There will be other ways of hearing God, of course, but the one thing that ties them all together is a heartfelt, if sometimes faltering, desire to put God at the centre of what I do and who I am.

Q. WHAT UNEXPECTED WISDOM HAVE YOU HEARD FROM FRIENDS AND COLLEAGUES WHO MAY NOT KNOW GOD?

Father God, alert me to the ways in which I can hear You speaking, knowing that You are likely to use things that I have been given me a natural affinity to. Help me to process what I hear and share with others to buld up Your church. Amen

---

... often people who, to my knowledge, have very little to do with God, can come out with words showing truly Godly insight ...

THE WORD OF GOD IS ALIVE AND ACTIVE

THE HEAVENS DECLARE THE GLORY OF GOD
THE SKIES PROCLAIM THE WORK OF HIS HANDS
Psalm 19:1

ALL THE TREES OF THE FOREST
WILL SING FOR JOY
Psalm 96:12

FAILURE TO LEARN FROM MISTAKES

ABRAHAM

17

ABRAHAM'S behaviour seems to swing around a lot! Following exemplary hospitality and bold bargaining with God, in Genesis 20, we find him up to his old trick of deception - almost a carbon copy of years gone by when he was in Egypt.

Here, it's King Abimelech who takes who he believes to be Abraham's sister, but discovers it is actually his wife, Sarah. After all his encounters with God and the extraordinary promises he had been given, this repeated deceit is surprising and disappointing.

Surprising, as you'd think that Abraham would have moved onto what you might call a higher plain.

Disappointing, as he'd not learned from what, previously, had clearly been a mistake.

We shouldn't be either surprised or disappointed, though, as God's work of transformation in us will take a lifetime. The "beast" of our old self may be chained up, but it can still roar at us.

If we don't realise this, we'll spend much time and energy beating up both ourselves and those around us, as we fail to meet our own heightened expectations. It's good that we are seeking to live in a manner more fitting of those who are now adopted members of God's family, but we must seek his empowering to change not rely on our own efforts.

It's back to the old paradox of faith and works.

Q. DO I HAVE A 'BESETTING SIN'? HAVE I SERIOUSLY BROUGHT IT BEFORE GOD FOR HIS HELP?

Father God, I so often despair of my apparent inablity to throw off my 'old self', being dragged down repeatedly by behaviours and attitudes I thought I'd left behind. Thank you that You are a God of transformation, and give me patience, but not inaction, as You undergo Your work in me. Amen.

GOD'S WORK OF TRANSFORMATION IN US WILL TAKE A LIFETIME

THE "BEAST" OF OUR OLD SELF MAY BE CHAINED UP BUT IT CAN STILL ROAR AT US

AT LAST: THE INTENDED HEIR

18

Q. WHAT DIFFERENCE TO MY LIFE DOES IT MAKE TRUSTING IN JESUS'S DEATH ON A CROSS?

Father God, please forgive me where I fail to act in a way that demonstrates I am trusting Your provision for all my needs and, instead, try to make things happen myself - often with a poor outcome. Grant me a greater level of faith that my behaviour might be more in line with my beliefs. Amen.

GOD HIMSELF WILL PROVIDE THE LAMB

WE come to the final chapter of Abraham's epic journey, one that has seen him travelling long distances to new lands, and ascending ever closer to God's throne of grace, as he worked out what a life of faith looked like. There's one huge test of his faith to come. A son, Isaac, is born to Abraham and Sarah, who are understandably thrilled: *Sarah said, "God has brought me laughter, and everyone who hears about this will laugh with me." Genesis 21:6* Hooray, we all cheer! But look what happens next:

Some time later God tested Abraham. He said to him, "Abraham!" "Here I am," he replied. Then God said, "Take your son, your only son, whom you love - Isaac - and go to the region of Moriah. Sacrifice him there as a burnt offering on a mountain I will show you." Early the next morning Abraham got up and loaded his donkey. He took with him two of his servants and his son Isaac. When he had cut enough wood for the burnt offering, he set out for the place God had told him about. Genesis 22:1-3

What must Abraham have made of this? There is nothing in the text to indicate that he challenged God. Quite the opposite, it appears; Abraham simply gets on with what God tells him to do, and his comment to his son, when quizzed about the sacrifice, suggests there was nothing "stiff upper lip" going on here. Abraham genuinely trusted that God was in charge, so he didn't flap. *"God himself will provide the lamb for the burnt offering, my son." Genesis 22:8*

A simple enough statement, but a "Holy of Holies" moment - one that resonates down through history to that greater day on Calvary, outside a city wall, where the faith of every one of us is put to the test.

Do you and I, when push comes to shove, believe that God's Son will rescue us? Abraham did; we should; and just as God's promise came good then, so it does for us today.

VERY OLD AGE

ABRAHAM

19

When they reached the place God had told him about, Abraham built an altar there and arranged the wood on it. He bound his son Isaac and laid him on the altar, on top of the wood. Then he reached out his hand and took the knife to slay his son. But the angel of the Lord called out to him from heaven, "Abraham! Abraham!" "Here I am," he replied. "Do not lay a hand on the boy," he said. "Do not do anything to him. Now I know that you fear God, because you have not withheld from me your son, your only son." Genesis 22:9-12

GOD DOESN'T GET BORED WITH US ONCE WE'RE PAST THE YEARS OF OUR EARTHLY PRIME

AS a brief epilogue, Sarah died at the age of 127, but Abraham married again, had further children, whom he blessed with gifts, and lived to the ripe old age of 175. Isaac was to be his heir and Abraham played his part in finding the wife, Rebekah, that God had set aside for his son. *Abraham was now very old, and the Lord had blessed him in every way.* Genesis 24:1

God doesn't get bored with us once we're past the years of our earthly prime. Whatever physical limitations we may experience, He is faithful and will continue to bless into the next generation. If we stay close to God, we can enjoy the privilege of being part of this process.

YOU HAVE NOT WITHHELD FROM ME YOUR SON, YOUR ONLY SON

Q. AM I EXPECTING GOD TO CONTINUE TO ME USE ME AS I GROW OLDER?

Father God, grant me energy and desire to serve You as I grow older. Help me to look outwards and upwards, using my expertise and experience to bless those who are following behind me - that they might be blessed and know greater fruitfulness in their lives, and that Your name might beglorified in me. Amen

PRAYING with ABRAHAM

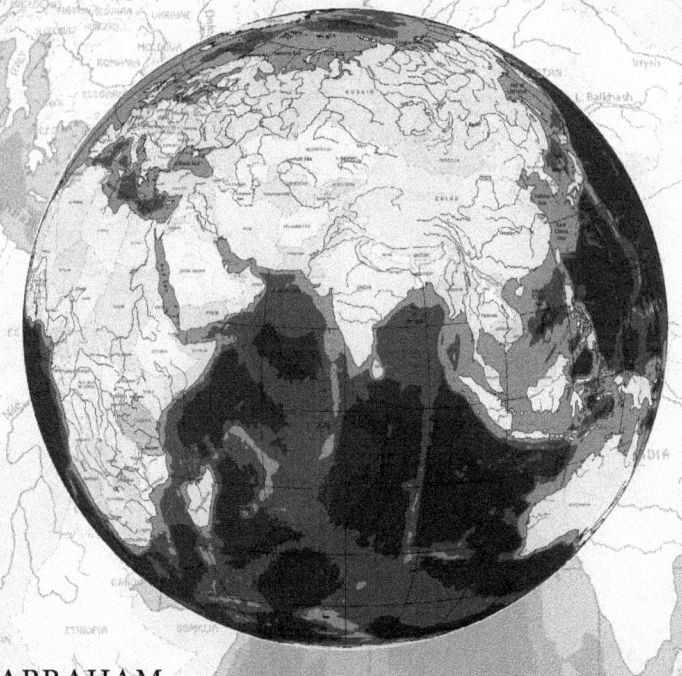

GOD OF ABRAHAM
who You named father of the nations,
grant us the faith and obedience that
Abraham demonstrated to take the gospel
of Jesus Christ to all peoples, whether they be
in or from distant lands, or our literal neighbour.
May we, like Abraham, be giving you the
praise and honour due to Your Name,
wherever we find ourselves.
Enable us to learn from his repeated
mistakes that we might walk in a
straight path every day of our lives.
Then may we know Your blessing until
and beyond our dying day.
Amen

> GRANT US
> THE FAITH AND
> OBEDIENCE
> ABRAHAM
> DEMONSTRATED

2 JESUS
king of kings

I umm-ed and ah-ed over whether to include Jesus as one of my 21 Bible Heroes. Clearly He is in the Bible - He's the initially unseen, but increasing visible focus of many of its 66 books. And clearly, to misquote Revelation (and Handel), He's the Superhero of Superheroes.

Yet, He's also God, albeit incarnate, and above all other names *(Philippians 2:9)*. And, to be honest, I'm just a little nervous that, when I meet Him face to face on That Glorious Day to come, He may raise an eyebrow at what I have said - assuming of course that He will have taken time out to read this book.

But I love Him and want the world to know a little about why that is. So, I'm going to risk His eybrow. Actually, it would be beyond ludicrous not to include Him. He is the focal person, not just of the Bible, but all of history.

Jesus, You're in.

I'm not going to attempt an overview of His life - read the gospels if you want that. In any case, it would be hopeless for, as the apostle John concluded his gospel:

Jesus did many other things as well. If every one of them were written down ... even the whole world would not have room for the books that would be written. John 21:25

How about this as a plan? Twenty one scenes from Jesus' life that speak of just why I love this Man. Agreed? Let's do it!

The challenge is restricting it to twenty one. The fun thing is: these are my favourites - you may have yours, but you can't argue with mine! The twenty one appear between each chapter, thus placing Jesus across everything. Neat.

A KING IS BORN
Matthew 2

JESUS #1

20

For to us a child is born, to us a son is given, and the government will be on his shoulders. And He will be called Wonderful Counsellor, Mighty God, Everlasting Father, Prince of Peace. Isaiah 9:6

After Jesus was born in Bethlehem in Judea, during the time of King Herod, Magi from the east came to Jerusalem and asked, "Where is the one who has been born king of the Jews? We saw his star when it rose and have come to worship him." Matthew 2:1-2

The fourth in line to the throne of England (above) faced an unknown future - even whether he'd ever actually make it to the throne - after all, when he ws born, his grandfather was still in the waiting room! The baby born in Bethlehem in the year that now divides history, knew his destiny from day one. He already was king of kings. He is a king I have no uncertainty about bowing my knee to.

Father God, awaken in me a real awareness that, in Christ, I am part of a royal priesthood, a member of a holy nation, belonging to God and called to declare His praises. *(1 Peter 2:9)* Amen

Q. DO I HAVE A SENSE OF SIGNIFICANT CALLING ON MY LIFE?

BARNABAS PUT THE 'CHRISTIAN' IN CHURCH

3 BARNABAS
benefactor & missionary

SON OF ENCOURAGEMENT — BARNABAS

THE first few chapters of Acts warm the heart. The newly established church in Jerusalem met frequently, engaging in powerful prayer, bold proclamation of the gospel, dramatic healing - all against a backdrop of praising the God who had recently raised Jesus from death.

Into this idyllic scenario walks Barnabas: ...

This is a good start, although Barnabas wasn't alone in this sacrificial giving, as we are told in the preceding few verses how all the believers shared everything they had. In applauding all this, it's tempting to think that it would have been easy for them to do that in those days, whereas today things are more complicated. But this won't do. Many of these people would have found themselves going without things we'd see as essential, being persecuted, brought before the authorities ... martyred.

It was as costly then as it will be today if we choose to live out gospel values. Sure, the challenges may be different, but the cost won't be. If we are to learn from the likes of Barnabas, we need to grapple with the tough stuff, as well as what we see as attractive.

Our next encounter with Barnabas is from a very different perspective. The arch persecutor of the early church, Saul, had undergone his Damascus Road experience and was now starting the difficult process of persuading those he had pursued that he was now a good guy. Not an easy task, but Barnabas stepped forward to support him: ...

This represented an important step in the rapid spread of the gospel through the region. A particular focus was the important commercial city of Antioch, where a great number of people believed and turned to the Lord.

And, yes, Barnabas re-appears: ...

BARNABAS TOOK SAUL AND BROUGHT HIM TO THE APOSTLES

Joseph, a Levite from Cyprus, whom the apostles called Barnabas - which means "son of encouragement" - sold a field he owned and brought the money and put it at the apostles' feet. Acts 4:36-37

But Barnabas took Saul and brought him to the apostles. He told them how Saul on his journey had seen the Lord and that the Lord had spoken to him, and how in Damascus he had preached fearlessly in the name of Jesus. Acts 9:27

Q. DO I MAKE IT MY BUSINESS TO BE AN ENCOURAGER?

Father God, set free the 'encourager' in me, that I might seek out those who need reassurance and come alongside them. Amen

BARNABAS AND SAUL

Q. AM I CONTENT PLAYING A SUPPORTING ROLE BESIDE THOSE IN THE LIMELIGHT?

... content to take second place ...
Colossians 3:12
(The Message)

Father God, open my eyes to see the needs of the Gospel in the situations I find myself in. Give me courage to step forward ... and indeed to step back when others take on the role I might have set in motion. Amen

HE SAW HOW GOD WAS USING THOSE AROUND HIM AND MADE SPACE FOR THEM TO FLOURISH

News of this reached the church in Jerusalem, and they sent Barnabas to Antioch. When he arrived and saw what the grace of God had done, he was glad and encouraged them all to remain true to the Lord with all their hearts. He was a good man, full of the Holy Spirit and faith, and a great number of people were brought to the Lord. Then Barnabas went to Tarsus to look for Saul, and when he found him, he brought him to Antioch. So for a whole year Barnabas and Saul met with the church and taught great numbers of people. The disciples were called Christians first at Antioch. Acts 11:22-26

WHAT an important figure Barnabas was. We see, as the story unfolds, that he was not one to push himself forward as the main man. Rather he always seemed happy to take a supporting role, particularly with Saul. But the significance of what he achieved cannot be overstated. He was a key player during the earliest days of the fledgling church, setting an example of what it means to live out faith in the context of fellowship - no lone ranger here.

He fearlessly came alongside the recent convert, Saul, to introduce him to the key players in the HQ church at Jerusalem. He was sent off to Antioch to support a major outbreak of the gospel - indeed of such note, that it was here that we read the name "Christian" was first used of the believers. Is it too much to say that Barnabas put the Christian in Church?!

Barnabas let none of this go to his head. He recognised his limitations by travelling north to get Saul to work alongside him. It's noteworthy that, at this point, the text reads "Barnabas and Saul" met with the church and taught them. This was soon to reverse to "Paul and Barnabas". Here was no clinger to power. He saw how God was using those around him, and made space for them to flourish.

BARNABAS CALLED

WE get a beautifully focused snapshot of the sort of man Barnabas was. He was glad to see the new Christians in Antioch, and encouraged them to hang on in there with all their hearts. "He was a good man, full of the Holy Spirit and faith." You can almost feel his warmth and humanity.

His running partner, Saul/Paul, was probably not so easy a character, but God, in His wisdom, brought together two very complementary personalities to ensure maximum impact for His work. Barnabas was an encourager - a wonderful thing to be and something we could all do with more of - and do more of ourselves. He also stimulated generosity and was completely trustworthy.

Whilst in Jerusalem, Barnabas would have experienced at first hand the persecution that broke out with James being executed and Peter locked up. But his role was to take the gospel to new territories and he returned with Saul to Antioch, where we next find him with the other church leaders:

While they were worshipping the Lord and fasting, the Holy Spirit said, "Set apart for me Barnabas and Saul for the work to which I have called them." So after they had fasted and prayed, they placed their hands on them and sent them off. The two of them, sent on their way by the Holy Spirit, went down to Seleucia and sailed from there to Cyprus. Acts 13:2-4

After a period of scuttling up and down the Eastern Mediterranean mainland, Barnabas and Saul come to a watershed moment as God directly intervenes to focus their energies. There's nothing everyday about Barnabas's call. It's in the context of fasting, prayer and worship and there is a clear sense of the Holy Spirit's presence and involvement. Indeed, the phase *"sent on their way by the Holy Spirit"* is most intriguing.

SET APART FOR ME BARNABAS AND SAUL FOR THE WORK TO WHICH I HAVE CALLED THEM

BARNABAS

The disciples, as each one was able, decided to provide help for the brothers and sisters living in Judea. This they did, sending their gift to the elders by Barnabas and Saul
Acts 11:29-30

Q. AM I WILLING TO STICK WITH A PARTNERSHIP WHERE THE PERSONALITIES ARE VERY DIFFERENT?

Father God, help me to be obedient to serve with whom you call me and in the tasks you have set for me ... with joy and gladness at all times. Amen

TO CYPRUS AND BEYOND

Q. AM I PREPARED TO SPEND SACRIFICIAL TIME WITH GOD TO HEAR HIS VOICE?

Father God, grow in me such a sense of trust in You that I am not easily put off when events unravel in a way that I had not expected or necessarily understand. Amen

IT'S enjoyable to imagine the church members cheering and waving goodbye as Barnabas and Saul are carried away in a whirlwind of fire! Unlikely maybe, but there is a real sense of supernatural calling and equipping, giving them and their senders a real sense of confidence and expectation.

If we want to have that same sense, we need to spend committed time, waiting on God and listening to Him. Is it significant that their first port of call is Cyprus, Barnabas's native land? It was the first time the gospel had crossed the sea and to have local knowledge of place, people and customs would have been invaluable as they travelled around Cyprus eventually reaching Paphos at the eastern end of the island.

There something happens: for the first time Saul starts being called Paul and thereafter, whenever their names are mentioned jointly (with a couple of exceptions). Barnabas, who previously was always listed first, now comes second.

Then, as they press on to mainland Turkey, their helper and Barnabas's cousin, John, leaves to return to Jerusalem. We hear more of this a while later as the two leaders plan to set out to revisit the churches they had earlier established.

So what happened in Paphos? The text doesn't tell us, but there is apparently some sort of "power shift", whereby Paul changes his name and takes over the leading role - which clearly doesn't suit John Mark. Barnabas, however seems prepared for this as he continues with Paul, even though he seems now to be the "junior" partner. Again, happy to take second place.

I would surmise that, had Barnabas shown the lack of maturity that John Mark did at this time (he was young and was later to write the gospel of Mark, so let's cut him some slack!), the story of the spread of the gospel might had read somewhat differently. Whatever the detail, it flags up that life and ministry can have their bumpy patches, but the faithful person, with a servant heart, will dust themselves down and get on with things, whatever their feelings at the time.

MIXED RECEPTION

BARNABAS

PAUL and Barnabas now tour around what is modern day Turkey and arrive at Pisidian Antioch. Their reception was polarised, many listened attentively, the disciples praised God, but ...

When the Jews saw the crowds, they were filled with jealousy. They began to contradict what Paul was saying and heaped abuse on him. Then Paul and Barnabas answered them boldly: "We had to speak the word of God to you first. Since you reject it and do not consider yourselves worthy of eternal life, we now turn to the Gentiles. Acts 13:45, 46

They soon found themselves thrown out of town and moved on to Iconium, where they had a similar response before arriving in Lystra where they met a different challenge. Paul healed a lame man and suddenly everyone wanted to treat Barnabas and him like gods. (How confused must Paul and Barnabas have been!)

When the crowd saw what Paul had done, they shouted in the Lycaonian language, "The gods have come down to us in human form!" Barnabas they called Zeus, and Paul they called Hermes because he was the chief speaker. ... but when the apostles Barnabas and Paul heard of this, they tore their clothes and rushed out into the crowd, shouting: "Friends, why are you doing this? We too are only human, like you. We are bringing you good news, telling you to turn from these worthless things to the living God, who made the heavens and the earth and the sea and everything in them. Acts 14:11,12,14,15

Whilst it was Paul who "performed" the healing - and it was him who the crowd soon tried to stone - Barnabas, seems to have led the response to the crowd, seeking to open their eyes to what was really going on.

TURN FROM THESE WORTHLESS THINGS TO THE LIVING GOD

Q. AM I ALERT TO THE NEED TO SUPPORT BY MY ACTIONS WHAT MY FELLOW BELIEVERS ARE SAYING AND DOING?

Father God, lead me into a 'deeper' discipleship, where I discern your mind through what I see with my eyes - though it may not be immediately obvious - and take actions accordingly. Amen

SINCE YOU REJECT THE WORD OF GOD AND DO NOT CONSIDER YOURSELVES WORTHY OF ETERNAL LIFE, WE NOW TURN TO THE GENTILES

SEASONED APOSTLE

26

Paul and Barnabas appointed elders for them in each church and, with prayer and fasting, committed them to the Lord, in whom they had put their trust.
Acts 14:23

Q. DO I TAKE TIME OUT TO STEP BACK FROM THE PRESSURES OF THE EVERYDAY TO DISCERN WHAT GOD IS DOING?

a prayer by Reinhold Niebuhr ...
Father God, grant me the serenity to accept the things I cannot change, courage to change the things I can, and wisdom to know the difference. Amen

BEING "a Barnabas" needs a particular skillset and personality. You need the gifting and charisma of a leader, but the gentleness, pragmatism and humility of a servant. If you strive to be the big cheese, there's nothing wrong with that, but you won't be a Barnabas. In reverse, you can still be a leader, without always having to be the one in the limelight.

Our friends move up the road to Derbe where they win a large number of disciples before returning to Antioch to report back and recharge their batteries. As they return, they revisit the places they had been, strengthening the new converts and establishing structures. I can envisage Barnabas doing much of the one to one encouragement, whilst Paul was putting the leadership framework in place.

Then, as now, issues of doctrine often threatened to divide the church. A sharp dispute about whether non Jewish converts needed to be circumcised was the issue of the day that saw Paul and Barnabas packed off to Jerusalem to hammer it out.

A number of those at HQ initially struggled to see that God had already been at work and was blessing the Gentiles. It took heated debate and persuasive argument to sort the issue out. Barnabas and Paul were crucial in helping the early church and its leaders to see that God was doing a new thing and they needed to catch up with it. As we look back we can see that Barnabas had grown from a committed, bold and caring member of the fledgling church into a seasoned apostle and leader under God. Not as high profile as the gospel writers or his long term partner in the field, Paul, but every bit as important in the establishment and early growth of the church and a tireless encourager of the faithful. A good man.

YOU CAN STILL BE A LEADER, WITHOUT ALWAYS HAVING TO BE THE ONE IN THE LIMELIGHT

PRAYING with BARNABAS

FATHER GOD
so much I see around me
flows from a culture where self is put at the centre.
As I look at Barnabas,
I see a man who was humble and such an encourager.

I am sorry where I go with the flow
and put myself in front of others.
Please set me free from self
and enable me to be "a Barnabas",
looking to the challenges faced by family, friends and colleagues
and giving them encouragement in all they do.

Open my eyes to the needs of those I can help.
Teach me to share what I have
without being fearful of losing out myself.
Help me to give with a joyful heart.

Please give me security in who you've made me,
and contentment with the tasks you set before me.
Protect me from envy of others
and set me free to give support
and a helping hand at all times. Amen

I AM SORRY WHERE I GO
WITH THE FLOW AND PUT
MYSELF IN FRONT OF OTHERS

WOMAN AT THE WELL
John 4

JESUS #2

27

When a Samaritan woman came to draw water, Jesus said to her, "Will you give me a drink?"…The Samaritan woman said to him, "You are a Jew and I am a Samaritan woman. How can you ask me for a drink?" John 4:7,9

Jesus answered, "Everyone who drinks this water will be thirsty again, but whoever drinks the water I give them will never thirst. Indeed, the water I give them will become in them a spring of water welling up to eternal life." John 4:13-14

Jesus uses an everyday encounter to seamlessly lead from idle gossip to life changing revelation. Brilliant!

Q. AM I PREPARED TO HAVE MY PRE-CONCEIVED NOTIONS OF HOW GOD ACTS TURNED ON THEIR HEAD?

Father God, give me boldness to stand up against the expectancy of contemporary culture to act in a way that Jesus would have done - with love at the heart. Amen

WOMAN CAUGHT IN ADULTERY #3
John 8

"Teacher, this woman was caught in the act of adultery. In the Law, Moses commanded us to stone such women. Now what do you say?" John 8:4-5

Jesus - the calm at the eye of every storm

Jesus asked her, "Woman, where are they? Has no one condemned you?" "No one, sir," she said. "Then neither do I condemn you," Jesus declared. "Go now and leave your life of sin." John 8:10-11

Jesus bent down and started to write on the ground with his finger. When they kept on questioning him, he straightened up and said to them, "Let any one of you who is without sin be the first to throw a stone at her." John 8:6-7

WE SHOULD GO UP AND TAKE POSSESSION
OF THE LAND, FOR WE CAN CERTAINLY DO IT

4 CALEB
team leader

JUST DO IT

CALEB

28

DO I absolutely love Caleb? Yes I do! He would have been the perfect advertising face of Nike - "Just do it."

Of the 12 leaders sent out to spy the land God had promised to the Israelites, only Caleb and Joshua urged the people to press on rather than turn away in fear at the challenges ahead: *Then Caleb silenced the people before Moses and said, "We should go up and take possession of the land, for we can certainly do it." Numbers 13:30*

Yet the people were scared, as its occupants seemed huge and invincible, and they were but grasshoppers by comparison. Fear quickly turned to disobedience and everything started to go pear-shaped. But, Caleb and Joshua weren't going to throw in the towel. Their response revealed an entirely different use of fabric.

Joshua son of Nun and Caleb son of Jephunneh, who were among those who had explored the land, tore their clothes and said to the entire Israelite assembly, "The land we passed through and explored is exceedingly good. If the Lord is pleased with us, he will lead us into that land, a land flowing with milk and honey, and will give it to us. Only do not rebel against the Lord. And do not be afraid of the people of the land, because we will devour them. Their protection is gone, but the Lord is with us. Do not be afraid of them." Numbers 14:6-9

Caleb responded differently to the rest of the people as he wanted to grasp the opportunity - "an exceedingly good land, flowing with milk and honey" - **rather than tremble at the threat** - "do not be afraid because we will devour them ... their protection is gone." Crucially - "the Lord is with us". But fear won the day and the people started grumbling. God wasn't impressed and told them so. If the people weren't prepared to trust Him for what they hadn't earned, they would reap the reward of their own fear.

The Lord said to Moses, "send some men to explore the land of Canaan, which I am giving to the Israelites. From each ancestral tribe send one of its leaders." So at the Lord's command Moses sent them out from the desert of paran. All of them were leaders of the Israelites. These are their names: ... from the tribe of Judah, Caleb son of Jephunneh. Numbers 13:1-6

Q. DO I REACT IN RESPONSE TO WHAT I BELIEVE BY FAITH OR WHAT I SEE WITH MY EYES?

Father God, I'd love to be a Caleb, but I don't always have the clarity of vision or boldness of word and deed to make it happen. Help me to be brave for You, so that Your Kingdom might grow. Amen

CALEB RESPONDED DIFFERENTLY TO THE REST OF THE PEOPLE AS HE WANTED TO GRASP THE OPPORTUNITY

THE LAND WE PASSED THROUGH
AND EXPLORED IS EXCEEDINGLY GOOD

JUST DO IT   CALEB

Nevertheless, as surely as I live and as surely as the glory of the Lord fills the whole earth, not one of those who saw my glory and the signs I performed in Egypt and in the wilderness but who disobeyed me and tested me ten times - not one of them will ever see the land I promised on oath to their ancestors.

But because my servant Caleb has a different spirit and follows me wholeheartedly, I will bring him into the land he went to, and his descendants will inherit it. ... Not one of you will enter the land I swore with uplifted hand to make your home, except Caleb son of Jephunneh and Joshua son of Nun. Numbers 14:21-24,30

CALEB (and Joshua), who had believed God's word, were to see what they had believed in by faith even though their eyes had suggested something different. Them and their descendants ... but none of the others ...

Of the men who went to explore the land, only Joshua son of Nun and Caleb son of Jephunneh survived. Numbers 14:38

For the Lord had told those Israelites they would surely die in the wilderness, and not one of them was left except Caleb son of Jephunneh and Joshua son of Nun. Numbers 26:65

As the Israelites wandered around the wilderness for 40 years, they continued to rail against God and His plans, even as they approached the Promised Land and started to see that it was actually pretty good - "suitable for livestock". God's response is interesting.

The Lord's anger was aroused that day and he swore this oath: 'Because they have not followed me wholeheartedly, not one of those who were twenty years old or more when they came up out of Egypt will see the land I promised on oath to Abraham, Isaac and Jacob - not one except Caleb son of Jephunneh the Kenizzite and Joshua son of Nun, for they followed the Lord wholeheartedly.' Numbers 32:10-12

> Q. IS MY COMMITMENT TO GOD SUCH THAT I DESIRE A DIFFERENT SPIRIT TO THOSE AROUND ME WHO DO NOT NAME JESUS AS LORD?

Father God, please help me to believe - to really believe - Your Word, and to live my life by it alone, rather than trying to pick and choose between Your paths and the way of the world. Amen

BUT, BECAUSE MY SERVANT CALEB HAS A DIFFERENT SPIRIT I WILL BRING HIM INTO THE LAND

WHOLEHEARTED

30

I WILL GIVE HIM AND HIS DESCENDANTS THE LAND HE SET HIS FEET ON, BECAUSE HE FOLLOWED THE LORD WHOLEHEARTEDLY
Deuteronomy 1:35-36

Q. DO I PRAY FOR WISDOM FOR THOSE CHOOSING LEADERS IN THE CHURCH?

Father God, fill me afresh each day with a desire to follow You wherever You lead - whether that be for four and a half years or 45, like Caleb. And may I be found as faithful as he was. Amen

NO ONE FROM THIS EVIL GENERATION SHALL SEE THE GOOD LAND I SWORE ... EXCEPT CALEB

THE word "wholeheartedly" makes a double appearance here and, for me, sums up why God blessed Caleb so greatly. I'm sure Caleb spotted the big bruisers who inhabited the land, and I've no doubt he looked them up and down with some trepidation. I'm also sure that Caleb wasn't a perfect man, and he no doubt disobeyed God on occasion (check out Romans 3:10 if you need convincing). But he didn't allow these things to stop him in his tracks. No, he pressed on - wholeheartedly - and tried to take those around with him.

We soon find Moses being commanded by God to make another selection of leaders, this time to take the land, not just give it the once over. The list still has twelve names, one representing each tribe, but only two are the same as before, Joshua and ... Caleb, who has moved to top of the list: *And appoint one leader from each tribe to help assign the land. These are their names: Caleb son of Jephunneh, from the tribe of Judah ... Numbers 34:18-19*

It's worth noting that the land Caleb was to have for himself and his descendants, was not some random gift or politically correct allocation, but that which he had set foot on. God responded to Caleb's integrity by giving him the territory he had shown faithfulness over, not anyone else's: *"No one from this evil generation shall see the good land I swore to give your ancestors, except Caleb son of Jephunneh. He will see it, and I will give him and his descendants the land he set his feet on, because he followed the Lord wholeheartedly." Deuteronomy 1:35-36*

45 years elapsed between Caleb's wholehearted commitment to God and the fulfilment of what was promised. That's a serious gap - particularly when you've spent the period between wandering endlessly round a wilderness with the very people who had undermined your confidence in God's plans. But the time did come, and Caleb's running mate, Joshua, had now taken over from Moses as leader.

85 YEARS OLD!

CALEB

Now the people of Judah approached Joshua at Gilgal, and Caleb son of Jephunneh the Kenizzite said to him, "You know what the Lord said to Moses the man of God at Kadesh Barnea about you and me. I was forty years old when Moses the servant of the Lord sent me from Kadesh Barnea to explore the land. And I brought him back a report according to my convictions, but my fellow Israelites who went up with me made the hearts of the people melt in fear. I, however, followed the Lord my God wholeheartedly.

So on that day Moses swore to me, 'The land on which your feet have walked will be your inheritance and that of your children forever, because you have followed the Lord my God wholeheartedly.' "Now then, just as the Lord promised, he has kept me alive for forty-five years since the time he said this to Moses, while Israel moved about in the wilderness.

So here I am today, eighty-five years old! I am still as strong today as the day Moses sent me out; I'm just as vigorous to go out to battle now as I was then. Now give me this hill country that the Lord promised me that day. You yourself heard then that the Anakites were there and their cities were large and fortified, but, the Lord helping me, I will drive them out just as he said."

Then Joshua blessed Caleb son of Jephunneh and gave him Hebron as his inheritance. So Hebron has belonged to Caleb son of Jephunneh the Kenizzite ever since, because he followed the Lord, the God of Israel, wholeheartedly. Joshua 14:6-14

JUST as vigorous at 85 as he was at 45. I'd like some of what he had, please! His drive and vigour are explained by four words tucked in at the end of his statement: "... the Lord helping me ..."

HE WAS JUST AS VIGOROUS AT 85 AS HE WAS AT 45
... THE LORD HELPING ME

Q. WHAT DO I CLASSIFY AS SUCCESS IN MY LIFE?

Father God, thank you for the example of those who have followed You faithfully down the centuries. May I be added to their number in my day - not due of my effort, but because my obedience to Your leading. Amen

LIVE THE LIFE

32

Q. HOW MUCH DO I STUDY THE LIVES OF THE SAINTS TO LEARN HOW GOD WORKED IN THEIR LIVES?

Teach me your way, Lord, that I may rely on your faithfulness; give me an undivided heart, that I may fear you name. Amen

CALEB was not a gung-ho maniac, who would charge at a bull without care for the consequence. He had heard God's promises, weighed them, and taken the decision to trust, even though the evidence of his eyes, and the pressure of those around him, was to do no such thing. The outcome was blessing and a precious inheritance. But not without serious effort and no doubt some set backs along the way.

As Moses had promised, Hebron was given to Caleb, who drove from it the three sons of Anak. Judges 1:20

So there he is; one of my biblical favourites. A wholehearted man whose focus was to live the life he believed he had been called to.

Never mind that he was swimming against the tide of popular opinion.

Never mind that the challenges that had driven others back, hadn't actually disappeared.

Never mind that decades passed before firm evidence emerged to show that God and His promises would come good.

Never mind that most of us would have been relaxing at home in retirement when the call came to take the land.

Never mind that it was tough - Caleb took the view that He would walk in God's path for his life, and he let nothing weaken his resolve or draw him away. He was a wholehearted follower of The Lord.

I want to be more like Caleb and, to this end, my prayer resonates with David in Psalm 86:11 *"Teach me your way, Lord, that I may rely on your faithfulness; give me an undivided heart, that I may fear you name"*. Amen

GIVE ME AN UNDIVIDED HEART

PRAYING with CALEB

FATHER GOD
thank you for Caleb,
a man who trusted You
in the face of much
faithlessness around him
and kept on believing
Your promises until old age.
Grant me his something of
Caleb's single mindedness,
determination, persistence,
wholeheartedness.

May my latter years on this Earth
be as energetically lived as Caleb's
and may I know Your enabling
power in my life,
as he did in his.
And may it be to the
glory of Your name,
Lord Jesus.
Amen

THE WIDOW'S MITE
Mark 12

33

JESUS #4

Many rich people threw in large amounts. But a poor widow came and put in two very small copper coins, worth only a few cents. Mark 12:41-42

Q. WHAT DO I REALLY VALUE IN LIFE?

Father God, lead me to give you my very best, even when it seems as if I cannot afford it. And may I do so, not to impress others, but in privacy, before You alone. Amen

THEY ALL GAVE OUT OF THEIR WEALTH; BUT SHE, OUT OF HER POVERTY, PUT IN EVERYTHING

Jesus said: "Truly I tell you, this poor widow has put more into the treasury than all the others. They all gave out of their wealth; but she, out of her poverty, put in everything - all she had to live on." Mark 12:43-44

No need to spell out why this is great!

TOWERS OF BABEL ARE ALIVE AND WELL TODAY!

5 DANIEL
overseas diplomat

NAME CHANGE

DANIEL

34

DANIEL has his own book in the Bible, which is pretty cool. We first encounter him as the mighty King Nebuchadnezzar sweeps in from the East to capture Jerusalem, Daniel's home town. Part of Neb's booty is a selection of young talent, who are whisked off to Babylon to serve in the king's palace.

Among those who were chosen were some from Judah: Daniel, Hananiah, Mishael and Azariah. The chief official gave them new names: to Daniel, the name Belteshazzar; to Hananiah, Shadrach; to Mishael, Meshach; and to Azariah, Abednego. Daniel 1:6-7

This is not a promising prospect for the young Daniel and his friends. And insult was soon added to injury, as his name was changed and he was forced to embark on a health spa lifestyle to make him fit for service. This included consuming royal food and wine, but Daniel resolved not to defile himself and he asked the chief official for permission to stick with his own diet.

Please test your servants for ten days: Give us nothing but vegetables to eat and water to drink. Then compare our appearance with that of the young men who eat the royal food, and treat your servants in accordance with what you see." So he agreed to this and tested them for ten days. At the end of the ten days they looked healthier and better nourished than any of the young men who ate the royal food. Daniel 1:12-15

As an indulgent, but hopefully entertaining aside, a few years back, I found myself called upon to read the opening chapter of Daniel in front of several hundred members of my home church. Verse 12 (underlined above) spanned two facing pages of the Bible in front of me and I heard myself saying "... test your vegetables ..." - I'd skipped a line at the end of the page! And this was way before Masterchef had even been thought of!

Q. HOW MUCH DO I FEAR SUFFERING FOR MY FAITH, AS DANIEL AND HIS FRIENDS DID?

Father God, please help me to see clearly what areas of my Christian walk are open to cultural flexibility, and which are non-negotiable. Amen.

COMPARE OUR APPEARANCE WITH THAT OF THE YOUNG MEN WHO EAT THE ROYAL FOOD

TRUSTWORTHY

I'M already impressed at Daniel. He didn't let adverse circumstances throw him off his path of faith. He trusted God to intervene in something relatively small and found himself upheld. Also interesting was that he didn't seem to kick up a fuss about his name change. He had already learned, even at his relatively tender age, to discern what was significant (and could be changed) and what wasn't. God was quick to honour this faithfulness and Daniel's exercise of his giftedness.

To these four young men God gave knowledge and understanding of all kinds of literature and learning. And Daniel could understand visions and dreams of all kinds. Daniel 1:17

Reminds me of Jesus' parable of the talents in Luke 19, where the master announces to the servant making good use of the investment he had received *'Because you have been trustworthy in a very small matter, take charge of ten cities.'*

This principle was soon to play out with Daniel, for King Neb started to have scary dreams, but his usual honchos couldn't tell him what they meant. Everyone was going to lose their heads, literally, until Daniel heard of the dilemma: *At this, Daniel went in to the king and asked for time, so that he might interpret the dream for him. ... During the night the mystery was revealed to Daniel in a vision. Daniel 2:16,19*

And so Daniel was able to discern the king's dream and the day was saved. He might have felt rather pleased with himself and taken a spot of credit, but Daniel knew the reality of the situation:

I thank and praise you, God of my ancestors: You have given me wisdom and power, you have made known to me what we asked of you, you have made known to us the dream of the king. Daniel 2:23

Q. DO I DESIRE GIFTING TO ENABLE ME TO SPEAK TRUTH INTO PEOPLE'S LIVES?

DANIEL COULD UNDERSTAND VISIONS AND DREAMS OF ALL KINDS

Father God, move me out of my comfort zone to engage with those around me about spiritual matters that are of significance to their eternal destiny. Amen

HIGH STAKES

DANIEL

GOD wasn't going to be outdone, though, and he immediately honoured Daniel: *Then the king placed Daniel in a high position and lavished many gifts on him. He made him ruler over the entire province of Babylon and placed him in charge of all its wise men. Moreover, at Daniel's request the king appointed Shadrach, Meshach and Abednego administrators over the province of Babylon, while Daniel himself remained at the royal court. Daniel 2:48-49*

Is there a hint of prosperity gospel here as Daniel and his four pals land well and truly on their feet - do right by God and reap the benefits? Turn the page though, and things take a swift left turn. King Neb gets a massively high image of himself made and everyone is ordered to bow the knee to it. Towers of Babel are alive and well today!

Daniel's three friends take a stand and find themselves taking the heat, only to be rescued from the flames by a mystery fellow furnace-walker generally reckoned to be no less than The Lord Jesus Himself.

I wonder where Daniel was at this time? Regardless, the three friends get themselves a further promotion. This is no prosperity gospel here. It's the principal of God placing growing responsibility in those who have shown themselves trustworthy.

Daniel meantime finds himself back interpreting Nebuchadnezzar's next dream - this time he is a high tree about to be felled and Daniel has to break the bad news that's Neb's time is up and that he's going to lose his throne and go mad before getting both his senses and throne back again. Not the easiest message to convey to an apparently all powerful king, but no one ever said that the path of faithful service was either easy or straightforward.

Q. DO I EXPECT EARTHLY REWARD FOR CARRYING OUT GOD'S WORK?

Father God, awaken in me a desire to serve you, whatever the cost and however difficult the situation it might place me in. Amen

THE KING PLACED DANIEL IN A HIGH POSITION

NO ONE EVER SAID THAT THE PATH OF FAITHFUL SERVICE WAS EITHER EASY OR STRAIGHTFORWARD

SPEAKING CLEARLY

Q. HAVE I EVER BEEN TEMPTED TO TAKE THE PRAISE FOR SOMETHING WHEN I KNEW GOD'S HAND LAY BEHIND IT?

Father God, warm my heart to be generous in my praise of others, keen to attribute good deeds to my brothers and sisters in Christ, and ready to declare the Gospel at all times. Amen.

SOMETIMES WE NEED TO SPEAK CLEARLY, ALBEIT HUMBLY, ABOUT THE GOSPEL

YET, I jump ahead prematurely, for part of Daniel's challenge was to make clear to the king what, or rather Who was the source of his gifting and the power that lay behind it. This is how the king reported what happened after his own sorcerers and magicians had failed to interpret his dream.

Finally, Daniel came into my presence and I told him the dream. (He is called Belteshazzar, after the name of my god, and the spirit of the holy gods is in him.) Daniel 4:8

So even though, after his first session of dream interpretation, Daniel had made quite clear who was responsible - *"... but there is a God in heaven who reveals mysteries. He has shown King Nebuchadnezzar what will happen in days to come." Daniel 2:28* - it takes time and a major life crisis for King Nebuchadnezzar to understand who this God really was.

Daniel approaches the matter with careful wording but a clear and courageous challenge to the king. *"... your kingdom will be restored to you when you acknowledge that Heaven rules. Therefore, Your Majesty, be pleased to accept my advice: Renounce your sins by doing what is right, and your wickedness by being kind to the oppressed. It may be that then your prosperity will continue." Daniel 4:26-27*

There's a balance to learn here, where we can assume our audience knows what we mean when we embark on "God talk", when in fact they may have a totally different picture. We need to listen carefully to what is actually being said to us and respond accordingly.
By contrast, we can pussyfoot around when sometimes we need to speak clearly, albeit humbly, about the gospel.

THERE IS A GOD IN HEAVEN
WHO REVEALS MYSTERIES

NEW REGIME: NEW CHALLENGES

DANIEL must have got it right as, having experienced what was foretold, we read: *"Now I, Nebuchadnezzar, praise and exalt and glorify the King of heaven, because everything he does is right and all his ways are just. And those who walk in pride he is able to humble. Daniel 4:37*

The story quickly moves on as a new king appears - Belshazzar. This time, Daniel is called on to interpret for the king mysterious writing on a wall during a banquet. "Call for Daniel, and he will tell you what the writing means", said the queen. Belshazzar's offer of gifts, if Daniel can interpret the writing, is rejected but Daniel gives an interpretation anyway, openly criticising the king's behaviour and concluding that his days are numbered. Which they were, as that very night he was slain. Daniel knew when to be gentle and choose his words carefully and when to be forthright and direct.

Next king on the scene is Darius the Mede, who's clearly heard of Daniel's reputation and puts him in a position of high authority. Those under him get jealous and we read that: *At this, the administrators and the satraps tried to find grounds for charges against Daniel in his conduct of government affairs, but they were unable to do so. They could find no corruption in him, because he was trustworthy and neither corrupt nor negligent. Finally these men said, "We will never find any basis for charges against this man Daniel unless it has something to do with the law of his God." Daniel 6:4,5*

Like many before and since, they resort to dirty tactics. Darius is tricked into making a daft edict, the result of which is that the king is horrified to find that the man he has trusted is thrown into a lion's den for openly praying to God and thereby transgressing his decree that no one should pray to a god or human but himself.

DANIEL

38

Q. DO I EXPECT PEOPLE TO RESPOND IF I SHARE THE GOOD NEWS ... OR AM I CYCNICAL THAT ANYTHING WILL COME OF IT?

Father God, please give me the courage to speak the truth to whoever You lead me to, regardless of whether they seem to welcome hearing it, or not. Amen

WE WILL NEVER FIND ANY BASIS FOR CHARGES AGAINST THIS MAN
... sounds like a dress rehearsal for Jesus' trial

LION TAMING

39

AS any diligent Sunday School child will know, Daniel remained unharmed and the king is delighted, throwing the very people who'd tricked him to the lions, who enjoy a good lunch. The king, like Nebuchadnezzar, eventually sees the error of his ways and does a U-turn.

"I issue a decree that in every part of my kingdom people must fear and reverence the God of Daniel. "For he is the living God and he endures forever; his kingdom will not be destroyed, his dominion will never end." Daniel 6:26

This episode is an eye opener: the king felt unable to overturn a clear injustice of his own making but, once Daniel is saved, he immediately turns on the culprits. Firm resolution dissolves into spiteful vengeance. By contrast Daniel, from the outset, identified the importance of what was going on, boldly put his trust in God and was justified. Man's 'strength' v faith's (apparent) 'weakness'.

Daniel's gift of insight then moves up a gear as we are given a window into his and our future. This is not the place for an analysis of Daniel's various visions, other than to observe that they involved the rise and fall of earthly kingdoms that came to pass in the centuries to follow, but also look forward to days yet to come.

God seems to give big visions to those in exile and it's not unreasonable to surmise that as the former happened as foretold, so will the latter.

Multitudes who sleep in the dust of the earth will awake: some to everlasting life, others to shame and everlasting contempt. Those who are wise will shine like the brightness of the heavens, and those who lead many to righteousness, like the stars for ever and ever. But you, Daniel, roll up and seal the words of the scroll until the time of the end. Many will go here and there to increase knowledge." Daniel 12:2-4

> Q. AM I PREPARED TO PUT MYSELF IN A PLACE OF POTENTIAL PAIN IF THERE IS THE CHANCE OF GAIN FOR GOD'S KINGDOM?

Father God, lift my eyes to see the eternal consequence of being bold for You - not just for others, but for myself as well. Amen

---

THOSE WHO ARE WISE WILL SHINE LIKE THE BRIGHTNESS OF THE HEAVENS

PRAYING with DANIEL

FATHER GOD
Daniel's commitment to You,
even, particularly, when times
were at their toughest,
is so admirable.
May we be prepared
to enter the lion's den
rather than deny You;
May we be prepared to stand
before leaders and tell the truth,
whatever the cost;
May we live disciplined lives
of prayer and worship
so that, when challenges come,
we are not caught unprepared
and give way to the pressures around us;
May we have a confidence that says
we will trust in You for the outcome,
even if it's not what we hope for;
May we be drawn deeper into Your ways
with each fresh revelation
of your faithfulness.
May we do all this
for Your glory. Amen

PREPARED TO TELL THE TRUTH
WHATEVER THE COST

CALMING THE STORM
Luke 8

40

JESUS #5

The disciples woke Jesus, saying, "Master, Master, we're going to drown!" He got up and rebuked the wind and the raging waters; the storm subsided, and all was calm. Luke 8:24

In fear and amazement they asked one another, "Who is this? He commands even the winds and the water, and they obey him. Luke 8:25

> Q. DO I LIFT UP TO JESUS MY TIMES OF PEACE AS WELL AS TURBULENCE?
>
> Lord Jesus come, please, and calm the storms that threaten to overturn my life.

#6

MARY & MARTHA
Luke 10

This is my summerhouse. I love spending time here in the quiet of our garden. As Jesus voted for Mary's peaceful calm, in preference to Martha's complaining busy-ness, I think he likes it when I sit here, as He has my full attention.

Mary sat at the Lord's feet listening to what he said. But Martha was distracted by all the preparations that had to be made. Luke 10:39-40

PEOPLE LOOK AT THE OUTWARD APPEARANCE
... BUT THE LORD LOOKS AT THE HEART

6 DAVID
shepherd, soldier, psalmist, king

LAST WILL BE FIRST

DAVID

41

THE New Testament starts thus: *"This is the genealogy of Jesus the Messiah, the son of David ..." Matthew 1:1* We are told that Jesus (Messiah, Saviour, Lord ... God) is the son of David (shepherd, lyre player, song writer ... adulterer). It's hard to comprehend. And David himself was far from a straight line. Lion slayer, giant killer, conqueror of many lands. But also bigamist, skimpily clad street dancer and run away. Complex character this; I like him.

How did David make such a heady transition from shepherd boy to king? Having first encountered him as the great grandson to come from the happy union of Boaz and Ruth (Ruth 4:12), we then find him as part of a talent line up to replace Israel's first king, Saul: *The Lord said to Samuel, "How long will you mourn for Saul, since I have rejected him as king over Israel? Fill your horn with oil and be on your way; I am sending you to Jesse of Bethlehem. I have chosen one of his sons to be king." 1 Samuel 16:1*

As the prophet Samuel hot foots it to Bethlehem, a procession of Jesse's tall and handsome sons are paraded before him. God had different ideas: *But the Lord said to Samuel, "Do not consider his appearance or his height, for I have rejected him. The Lord does not look at the things people look at. People look at the outward appearance, but the Lord looks at the heart." 1 Samuel 16:7*

Seven sons are rejected and Samuel is concerned, so he asked Jesse: *"Are these all the sons you have?" "There is still the youngest," Jesse answered. "He is tending the sheep." Samuel said, "Send for him; we will not sit down until he arrives." 1 Samuel 16:11*

Does it seem odd that God chose the apparently least, rather than the obvious? Maybe not, as Saul, who was to be deposed as king had been head and shoulders above those around him, but it turned out that brawn was not might. His heart was not turned to God and he was disobedient.

Q. WHAT IS THE BASIS ON WHICH I WOULD CHOOSE PEOPLE FOR JOBS THAT NEED DOING IN THE CHURCH?

A HEADY TRANSITION FROM SHEPHERD BOY TO KING

Father God, help me to understand better that you have chosen me to be your servant, because of your love and grace, not my merits. As you used David, with all his imperfections, use me to further your Kingdom in this, my day. Amen

I AM SENDING YOU TO JESSE OF BETHLEHEM I HAVE CHOSEN ONE OF HIS SONS TO BE KING

NOT ALL AS IT SEEMS

42

Q. HOW MUCH AM I INCLINED TO JUDGE PEOPLE BY FIRST APPEARANCES?

Father God, open my eyes to see the people I meet each day as you view them, helping me to judge each person's true potential, and contribute to their growth. Amen

THE LORD WHO RESCUED ME FROM THE PAW OF THE LION AND THE PAW OF THE BEAR WILL RESCUE ME FROM THE HAND OF THIS PHILISTINE

THEN the word of the Lord came to Samuel: *"I regret that I have made Saul king, because he has turned away from me and has not carried out my instructions."*
1 Samuel 15:10-11

The position is quite clear. God looks at the unseen heart, not the outward appearance. In context, "appearance" clearly refers to suitability, not just whether you are good looking or not, for we read: *So Samuel sent for David and had him brought in. He was glowing with health and had a fine appearance and handsome features.*

Then the Lord said, *"Rise and anoint him; this is the one." So Samuel took the horn of oil and anointed him in the presence of his brothers, and from that day on the Spirit of the Lord came powerfully upon David.*
1 Samuel 16:12-13 Wow! Transformed in a matter of minutes from unknown shepherd boy to king-in-waiting. And, what's more, filled with an unstoppable power to deliver. But, of course, the unknown shepherd boy had been learning a lot out in the fields of his youth that would prepare him for what lay ahead.

We read a little later, as David was explaining to King Saul why the giant Goliath should not be feared: *"Your servant has been keeping his father's sheep. When a lion or a bear came and carried off a sheep from the flock, I went after it, struck it and rescued the sheep from its mouth. When it turned on me, I seized it by its hair, struck it and killed it. Your servant has killed both the lion and the bear; this uncircumcised Philistine will be like one of them, because he has defied the armies of the living God. The Lord who rescued me from the paw of the lion and the paw of the bear will rescue me from the hand of this Philistine."*
1 Samuel 17:34-37

GOD LOOKS AT THE UNSEEN HEART
NOT THE OUTWARD APPEARANCE

TO BE TRUSTED

DAVID

TAKE a look at the top picture here. There's no way that simple skill and strength would see off this bad boy. Clearly, David was given a divine hand even before we read that the Spirit of the Lord came powerfully on him when he was anointed by Samuel.

The imagery too - keeping his father's sheep - is just too coincidental. It is as if God, who must so enjoy planning all this stuff, was giving David a practice run on the hillside before calling him forward to the front line to look after his Father's sheep, as leader of Israel. David showed that he could be trusted with the smaller things, so God then moved him onto the bigger stage.

And on the bigger stage we next find him. The Spirit of God had left King Saul; we know it had transferred to David on his anointing, but Saul didn't, and an evil spirit had moved in and was tormenting him. Help was needed and the call went out for a musician to calm the king's nerves.

One of the servants answered, "I have seen a son of Jesse of Bethlehem who knows how to play the lyre. He is a brave man and a warrior. He speaks well and is a fine-looking man. And the Lord is with him." 1 Samuel 16:18

Enter David, musician and psalmist. Saul immediately likes him, and he enters the king's service as an armour bearer. *Whenever the spirit from God came on Saul, David would take up his lyre and play. Then relief would come to Saul; he would feel better, and the evil spirit would leave him. 1 Samuel 16:23*

Even as he's emerging from obscurity, we can see the different facets of David's character and giftedness. Brave fighter and mood changing musician. Gentle carer of sheep and spiritual warrior. No wonder the Psalms he wrote are so rich in contrast and emotion.

EVEN AS HE'S EMERGING FROM OBSCURITY, WE CAN SEE THE DIFFERENT FACETS OF DAVID'S CHARACTER AND GIFTEDNESS

Q. CAN I SEE THE BIGGER PICTURE OF WHAT GOD IS DOING IN MY LIFE? CAN I HELP OTHERS TO SEE IT IN THEIR LIVES?

Father God, enable me to do well those smaller things you want to see me carry out faithfully, that I may prove trustworthy for greater things in Your Kingdom. Amen

SPIRITUAL BATTLE

Q. HOW DO I SEE BEHIND THE OBVIOUS TO DISCERN IF THERE IS A SPIRITUAL CAUSE?

THERE'S A SPIRITUAL BATTLE ALL ABOUT US

Father God, grant me the discipline to put on Your full armour at all times that I might be ready for difficult times when they come so I am able to remain standing. Amen

SOON, though, it all turns sour with King Saul. Ironically, it comes about as a result of David doing well. Saul is so impressed at David's fearless flooring of the giant Goliath, that he quickly promotes him to high rank in his army, where David continues to be a success. But when the king hears the people singing *"Saul has slain his thousands, and David his tens of thousands." 1 Samuel 18:7*

Saul becomes angry and, as David plays for him during his next bout of depression, he unsuccessfully hurls a spear at his comforter. Ouch!

Isn't that just the way things can be. Everything's going well and then suddenly, apparently without reason, the wheels fall off, and you're wondering what it's all about. But a clue is given as to the cause here. An evil spirit came on Saul that turned his jealousy into murderous intent.

There's a spiritual battle all about us, with God on one side and the Devil on the other. Those filled with the Spirit of God, and daring to exercise the power it gives them - David in this instance - will find themselves opposed by the forces of evil. Although it may appear that people are on our case, it is actually unseen forces behind them that are the source.

The apostle Paul knew all about this, as he recorded for us a thousand years later: *For our struggle is not against flesh and blood, but against the rulers, against the authorities, against the powers of this dark world and against the spiritual forces of evil in the heavenly realms. Ephesians 6:12*

Paul's solution? *Therefore, put on the full armour of God, so that when the day of evil comes, you may be able to stand your ground, and after you have done everything, to stand. Ephesians 6:13*

PUT ON THE FULL ARMOUR OF GOD

SOUL MATE

DAVID

45

DAVID'S solution? He wrote Psalms expressing his challenges and frustrations at evil doers - eg Psalm 64: *They shoot from ambush at the innocent; they shoot suddenly, without fear. (v4) But God will shoot them with his arrows; they will suddenly be struck down. (v7)*

It's instructive to compare the two approaches - David sees bad stuff happen and invokes God's direct intervention. Paul, following the coming of the Holy Spirit at Pentecost, sees what's going on behind the scenes and prays for prevention and protection ... rather than retribution once it's happened. We, like Paul, are living in the Age of the Spirit and, if we are immersed in God's Word and engaged in His presence, we should be in a better position to anticipate challenges, rather than just reacting to them.

Meanwhile, David's situation deteriorates: *Saul was afraid of David, because the Lord was with David but had departed from Saul. 1 Samuel 18:12* However, in an increasingly difficult situation, God provides support and comfort for David in the person of Saul's son: *Jonathan became one in spirit with David ... and Jonathan made a covenant with David because he loved him as himself. Jonathan took off the robe he was wearing and gave it to David, along with his tunic, and even his sword, his bow and his belt. 1 Samuel 18:1,3-4*

How unexpectedly great is this; a soul mate for David, who must have seen Jonathan as a lifeline, as his father became increasingly paranoid and violent towards himself. In light of the apparent intimacy that develops between the two, there are those who have speculated whether it was a gay relationship. There is nothing to suggest that it was. Indeed, in light of the clear prohibition of homosexual relationships in the Old Testament and the fact that, later on in his story through the prophet Nathan, David is confronted by God over his (again prohibited) adultery with Bathsheba, this hypothesis seems very unlikely.

Q. DO I HAVE A SOUL MATE WHO I CAN TURN TO AT ANY TIME TO SHARE MY GREATEST CHALLENGES? IF NOT, SHOULD I?

Father God, thank you for the gift of friendship. Help me cultivate friendships that will strenghten me and to be available to others to support them. Amen

JONATHAN MADE A COVENANT WITH DAVID BECAUSE HE LOVED HIM AS HIMSELF

COMPLEX LOVE LIFE

Q. DO I UNDERSTAND MY OWN PERSONALITY WITH ITS VARIED NEEDS AND PREFERENCES?

Father God, help me to be aware of the snares that some try to set before me that I may avoid them and live a simple and pure life that glorifies You. Amen

TO BE FULLY HUMAN, AND THE PERSON GOD HAS MADE US, WE MUST LEARN TO IDENTIFY AND EMBRACE ALL OUR CONTRASTING CHARACTERISTICS

EQUALLY clearly, it flags up that it is both helpful and healthy for men to have strong and close relationships with each other. Watching a documentary about Alaskan grisly bears recently, the males seem to be defined by their aggression towards each other. But that is the animal kingdom, and does not need to be played out in human relationships.

David must have struggled to balance his creative and warrior instincts, both of which were strongly present. Our creativity will tend to draw us towards each other. The Warrior Within will pull in the opposite direction.

David's Psalms reveal his struggle to reconcile these in one personality. God Himself is variously portrayed in the Bible as Creator, Warrior, Father, Mother ... and we are made in His image. To be fully human, and the person God has made us, we must learn to identify and embrace all our contrasting characteristics.

We soon find out that David's love life was not to be straight forward. It starts out with Saul trying to trap David, first by offering his older daughter in marriage ... which David declined. But he was persistent:

Now Saul's daughter Michal was in love with David, and when they told Saul about it, he was pleased. "I will give her to him," he thought, "so that she may be a snare to him and so that the hand of the Philistines may be against him." So Saul said to David, "Now you have a second opportunity to become my son-in-law." 1 Samuel 18:20-21

David, even though he was filled with the Spirit, was unable to see through what was going on and he married Michal, who was to be a thorn in his side. Next we hear of her, she is placing an idol in David's bed whist helping him escape Saul's murderous plans. A while later, David is marrying still more wives and taking a bevvy of concubines - whilst Michal is married off to someone else.

ON THE RUN

DAVID

47

IT hardly seems surprising that Michal taunts David, as he dances before the ark when it enters Jerusalem, or that, later on, David commits adultery. Having a selection of wives may have been common practice in the culture of the day, but surely God's plan for relationships was one man, one woman, so this must have fallen outside God's plan? I don't understand this. Did God have a moratorium on worrying about this at that point in history?

And we soon discover David on the run from Saul, hiding in fields and pretending he's going mad, as he seeks to evade the increasingly dangerous king: *So he pretended to be insane in their presence; and while he was in their hands he acted like a madman, making marks on the doors of the gate and letting saliva run down his beard. 1 Samuel 21:13*

What's going on here? God's anointed, filled with the Spirit, a pivotal member of the royal line that would see God Himself walking on Earth. And yet, he's living in bigamy, on the run, surviving by deceit.

Surely David was not living a life of faith, trusting in his God? And yet we are later told that his heart was fully devoted to God and he followed the Lord completely.

As Solomon grew old, his wives turned his heart after other gods, and his heart was not fully devoted to the Lord his God, as the heart of David his father had been. ... so Solomon did evil in the eyes of the Lord; he did not follow the Lord completely, as David his father had done. 1 Kings 11:4,6

David's behaviour doesn't actually sound much different from his revered forbear Abraham, who slept with his slave girl, was on the run, and sought to live by deceit when the chips were down. And yet Abraham gets the longest mention in the Hebrews 11 Faith Hall of Fame.

Q. DO I JUDGE PEOPLE WHO SEEM TO BE DOING ALL THE WRONG THINGS? OR CUT THEM SOME SLACK UNTIL I UNDERSTAND BETTER HOW GOD MIGHT BE AT WORK IN THEM?

Father God, help me to understand that Your ways are not our ways and that you might be working your purposes out in the people I see around me in a way that is not always obvious. Amen

---

HE'S LIVING IN BIGAMY, ON THE RUN, SURVIVING BY DECEIT

PRIORITIES

Q. WHAT ARE THE MAIN PRIORITIES IN MY LIFE?

Father God, help me to surrender my whole life to You ... again and again, as I get to understand better what being 'in Christ' might look like in my life. Amen

DAVID, FOR ALL HIS FAILINGS, SEEMED TO HAVE HAD HIS HEART IN THE RIGHT PLACE AND WE WOULD DO WELL TO PRIORITISE OUR RELATIONSHIP WITH GOD OVER TRYING TO DO THE RIGHT THING

LET'S grapple with this. A key to understanding David's mindset may lie in his encounter with Goliath. His language and approach were military, albeit that he drew strength from his confidence that God was on his side: *"Who is this uncircumcised Philistine that he should defy the armies of the living God?" 1 Samuel 17:26*

"The Lord who rescued me from the paw of the lion and the paw of the bear will rescue me from the hand of this Philistine." 1 Samuel 17:37

I'm guessing that, at this stage in his life, David was aware of God's presence as a power that enabled him to do amazing things. As the apostle Paul would later recognise: *I can do all things through him who gives me strength. Philippians 4:13*

David was an empowered man of action. And he was quite prepared to give the glory to God for his success. But had he surrendered to God his whole life, with all it's day to day challenges? The fact that David took things into his own hands, apparently without enquiring of God, suggests not. Yet we find him commended as having a heart fully devoted to God. This would be perplexing, except we are dealing with a God of grace who knows our weaknesses and failings, yet loves us and blesses us regardless.

The issue at stake is not whether we get everything right, rather if we have an underlying trust in God. David, for all his failings, seemed to have had his heart in the right place and we would do well to prioritise our relationship with God over trying to do the right thing.

If that sounds odd, the message is that, if we put God first, other stuff will fall into place. If we strive to do our best, we will become proud if we succeed and downhearted if we fail. Whichever, God will be squeezed out.

IF WE PUT GOD FIRST, OTHER STUFF WILL FALL INTO PLACE

I REST AND REFLECT ON A WEARYING DAY ...
TAKING REFUGE IN THE SHADOW OF YOUR WINGS

Psalm 36:7

THE RIGHT THING

DAVID

49

WE move into ever more complicated territory as we track through David's story. Next up, he's crashing in on a priest asking for bread for his hungry men outside. There's an uncanny parallel with Jesus feeding the 5,000: *Now then, what do you have on hand? Give me five loaves of bread, or whatever you can find." 1 Samuel 21:3*

And the link to Jesus continues as Jesus quotes this episode - 1,000 years later - to Jews of the day who are getting all legalistic with him about picking ears of corn on the Sabbath: *Jesus answered them, "Have you never read what David did when he and his companions were hungry? He entered the house of God, and taking the consecrated bread, he ate what is lawful only for priests to eat. And he also gave some to his companions." Then Jesus said to them, "The Son of Man is Lord of the Sabbath." Luke 6:3-5*

Pardon the pun, but David, like his "Greater Son", could separate the wheat from the chaff. His closeness of relationship to God enabled him to instinctively know what was the right thing in God's eyes. In this case, it was more important to meet a human need rather than sticking to the letter of the law.

We now follow David through a series of unsavoury incidents as he flees from King Saul. Whole towns are put to the sword as the increasingly crazy king hunts his quarry.

David, by contrast, seems to be getting into the swing of consulting with God before taking action: *When David was told, "Look, the Philistines are fighting against Keilah and are looting the threshing floors," he inquired of the Lord, saying, "Shall I go and attack these Philistines?" The Lord answered him, "Go, attack the Philistines and save Keilah." 1 Samuel 23:1-2*

Q. AM I GROWING EVER CLOSER TO GOD?

Father God, I want to do the right thing, but too often get it wrong. Draw me closer to You that I might learn Your ways so they become increasingly instinctive to me. Amen

DAVID'S CLOSENESS OF RELATIONSHIP TO GOD ENABLED HIM INSTINCTIVELY TO KNOW WHAT WAS THE RIGHT THING

PERFECT IN WEAKNESS

Q. DO I FEEL COMFORTABLE WITH WEAKNESS AND UNDERSTAND THAT IT PROVIDES SPACE FOR GOD'S GRACE?

Father God, keep me at peace as I walk through difficult times. Guard my heart and my mind, that I might continue to trust in You, whatever the challenge, whatever the outcome. Amen

WHEN I AM WEAK THEN I AM STRONG

IN this time of weakness, David has learned to trust God, whereas previously, with the rashness of youth and inexperience, he had almost seemed to take Him for granted.

The apostle Paul also knew all about this as he grappled with his thorn in the flesh: *Three times I pleaded with the Lord to take it away from me. But he said to me, "My grace is sufficient for you, for my power is made perfect in weakness." Therefore I will boast all the more gladly about my weaknesses, so that Christ's power may rest on me. That is why, for Christ's sake, I delight in weaknesses, in insults, in hardships, in persecutions, in difficulties. For when I am weak, then I am strong. 2 Corinthians 12:8-10*

As I write, I am passing through some weeks of testing in my workplace. Very stressful and upsetting, with many sleepless nights and day after day of worry as the outcome of my labours remains unknown. One of the first Bible verses I learned as a Christian was:

Do not be anxious about anything, but in every situation, by prayer and petition, with thanksgiving, present your requests to God. And the peace of God, which transcends all understanding, will guard your hearts and your minds in Christ Jesus. Philippians 4:6-7

I have tried to cling onto this promise - it's not easy, as anyone knows who has experienced times of testing - and I have yet to learn to rejoice in weakness. But I have sought the hand of Jesus as I walk through this particular valley, and trust that I will start to see how He has held me through these days.

MY GRACE IS SUFFICIENT FOR YOU, FOR MY POWER IS MADE PERFECT IN WEAKNESS

WAR AND PEACE

DAVID

51

AS an aside at this point, the whole context of life in 'those days' seemed to revolve around going to war, which rather grates compared with the Son of David's title, "Prince of Peace".

It's tempting, in the relatively peaceful 21st Century Western world, to think that humanity has moved on except, if memory serves me correct, there were more wars going on across the World in the 20th Century than ever before in history, including two World Wars.

Oh what a glorious day it will be when the historic City of David hands over to the New Jerusalem as the Holy City descends from Heaven with God revealing Himself in Person: *'He will wipe every tear from their eyes. There will be no more death or mourning or crying or pain, for the old order of things has passed away." Revelation 21:4 For now we see only a reflection as in a mirror; then we shall see face to face. Now I know in part; then I shall know fully, even as I am fully known. 1 Corinthians 13:12*

What a prospect. If that's "pie in the sky when you die", I'll have mine with ice cream, cream and custard please!

Back to David ... who soon has a bizarre opportunity to overcome his adversary, as Saul nips into a cave to "relieve himself" (love it, right there in the Bible) and chance has it (!) that it's the very same cave that David and his men are hiding from him.

The men said, "This is the day the Lord spoke of when he said to you, 'I will give your enemy into your hands for you to deal with as you wish.' " Then David crept up unnoticed and cut off a corner of Saul's robe. Afterward, David was conscience-stricken for having cut off a corner of his robe. 1 Samuel 24:4-5

Q. DO I LIVE MY LIFE IN THE CONTEXT OF A NEW HEAVEN AND NEW EARTH BEING 'ON THEIR WAY'?

Father God, help me to be a person of peace, however great the provocation and however tempting it might be to take things into my own hands. That Your name might be glorified on Earth as it is in Heaven. Amen

THERE WILL BE NO MORE DEATH
OR MOURNING OR CRYING OR PAIN

CREATIVE SOLUTION

Q. AM I HAPPY TO BE ACCUSED OF BEING WEAK BECAUSE I CHOOSE THE WAY OF RECONCILIATION?

Father God, grant me patience to continue 'doing the right thing' even though I might not see the end of the tunnel in times of insecurity, and uncertainly about Your plans for my life. Amen

MAY THE LORD REWARD YOU WELL FOR THE WAY YOU TREATED ME TODAY

THIS is the stuff of cartoons. Except that it's deadly serious. We're confronted with the dilemma of how to deal with "Free Will".

David, as his men confront him, can deal with the king as he wishes. How will he use his knife - to kill?

In an instinctive reaction (it wouldn't have taken long for Saul to relieve himself), David comes up with a creative solution. He uses the knife in his hand to cut off a corner of cloth and thus transform what could have been a national crisis of regicide to an opportunity for reconciliation.

Man or mouse? Clearly his men plumped for mouse, but David rounds on them: *"The Lord forbid that I should do such a thing to my master, the Lord's anointed, or lay my hand on him; for he is the anointed of the Lord."* 1 Samuel 24:6   A genius moment.

This conversation must have been carried in sign language, as it's only then that Saul leaves the cave and David runs out into the daylight to reveal to the king what had happened and plead for an end to his pursuit of him. Saul may be lurching in and out of paranoia, but he has a moment of clarity as he responds to David:

When a man finds his enemy, does he let him get away unharmed? May the Lord reward you well for the way you treated me today. I know that you will surely be king and that the kingdom of Israel will be established in your hands. 1 Samuel 24:19-20

As David continues to run and fight, there follows a series of wanderings in the wilderness. Is this a necessary stage for any great leader under God? Abraham, Moses, Joshua, Jesus, all had "wilderness times" before embarking on their ministry.

WISDOM AND FOLLY

DAVID

53

IS it in "the wilderness", a place of loneliness and danger, that God can best prepare his servants? As an example, there is an extraordinary encounter with Abigail, wise wife of the foolish Nabal, who wants to pick a fight with David, who in turn is about to rise to the bait. Abigail plunges into the breach:

Even though someone is pursuing you to take your life, the life of my lord will be bound securely in the bundle of the living by the Lord your God, but the lives of your enemies he will hurl away as from the pocket of a sling. When the Lord has fulfilled for my lord every good thing he promised concerning him and has appointed him ruler over Israel, my lord will not have on his conscience the staggering burden of needless bloodshed or of having avenged himself. And when the Lord your God has brought my lord success, remember your servant." 1 Samuel 25:29-31

David did stay his hand and did remember. A few days later, Nabal was struck down dead by God and David married Abigail! In an age of militarism and swift revenge, David had learned to listen to wise counsel. In a male dominated culture, he had followed the advice of a woman.

Soon the pursuit was over, as Saul takes his own life on the battlefield. You'd have thought that David would have celebrated in sheer relief. But when he received the report from a battlefield escapee, who thought he could get in David's good books by saying he'd killed the king, David's response was both startling and lethal: *David asked him, "Why weren't you afraid to lift your hand to destroy the Lord's anointed?" Then David called one of his men and said, "Go, strike him down!" So he struck him down, and he died. For David had said to him, "Your blood be on your own head. Your own mouth testified against you when you said, 'I killed the Lord's anointed.'"* 2 Samuel 1:14-16

Q. HOW MUCH WEIGHT DO I GIVE TO THE VOICE OF MEN COMPARED WITH WOMEN? - REGARDLESS OF WHICH GENDER I AM MYSELF

Father God, Your word says that 'the fear of the Lord is the beginning of wisdom'. Grant me wisdom to take right decisions in all I do, and not allow my emotions to take control. Amen

DAVID HAD LEARNED TO LISTEN TO WISE COUNSEL

EMERGING STATESMAN

Q. HOW GOOD AM I AT BEING PATIENT AND WAITING ON THE LORD'S TIMING? AND, IF NOT, WHAT AM I GOING TO DO ABOUT IT?

Father God, show me how I can act like a statesman in the situation you have placed me in - that Your plans might be given space to unfurl in Your timing. Amen

DAVID INQUIRED OF THE LORD

WITH his adversary out of the way, David might have immediately stepped forward as king. But we read otherwise:

In the course of time, David inquired of the Lord. "Shall I go up to one of the towns of Judah?" ... The Lord said, "Go up." David asked, "Where shall I go?" "To Hebron," the Lord answered. So David went up there with his two wives, Ahinoam of Jezreel and Abigail, the widow of Nabal of Carmel. David also took the men who were with him, each with his family, and they settled in Hebron and its towns. Then the men of Judah came to Hebron, and there they anointed David king over the tribe of Judah. When David was told that it was the men from Jabesh Gilead who had buried Saul, he sent messengers to them to say to them, "The Lord bless you for showing this kindness to Saul your master by burying him. 2 Samuel 2:1-4

Not only did David bide his time and do things in an orderly fashion, he took trouble to thank those who had given Saul a decent burial. Are we already seeing a statesman emerging here, instead of the impetuous warrior of earlier years?

Yet, in spite of David's graciousness, things were getting complicated. Saul's supporters put forward his son, Ish-Bosheth, as king of Israel and war breaks out: *The war between the house of Saul and the house of David lasted a long time. David grew stronger and stronger, while the house of Saul grew weaker and weaker. 2 Samuel 3:1*

After more argy-bargy, Ish-Bosheth is murdered although, like a cat bringing a dead bird into the kitchen hoping for praise, the murderers make the same mistake as the announcer of Saul's death and present Ish-Bosheth's severed head to David - who is incensed and has them promptly killed.

KING AT LAST

DAVID

55

DAVID'S life appears almost bizarre in its contrasts. He demonstrates great loyalty to a king who spent years trying to kill him, yet has several wives and is soon to steal another man's and have him killed. He is surrounded by loyal followers and yet is at war with half the kingdom. He is ruthless in having people he sees as traitors summarily executed and yet in his Psalms we find him pouring out his heart to God.

I don't understand all the ebbs and flows of David's life, but it does give an insight to the ups and downs we will encounter, if we try and live life to the full and commit ourselves wholeheartedly to God. There will be many pressure points and we won't get them all right. It will often be internally uncomfortable and externally confusing to those looking on.

However, rather than try to live a safe life without risk, if David's example is anything to go by, it seems that God calls us to step out and face whatever consequences may follow, even if some are of our own making where we get it wrong.

In this context, the only real failure is failure to try. But his time has come at last. David is made King of Israel, and his reign for real commences. Here are the stats:

David was 30 years old when he became king, and he reigned 40 years. In Hebron he reigned over Judah 7 years and 6 months, and in Jerusalem he reigned over all Israel and Judah 33 years. 2 Samuel 5:4-5

David's first major act as king is to take Jerusalem and make it his capital city. Here's how it happened: *The king and his men marched to Jerusalem to attack the Jebusites, who lived there. The Jebusites said to David, "You will not get in here; even the blind and the lame can ward you off." ... Nevertheless, David captured the fortress of Zion ...*

Q. DO I OPT FOR A SAFE LIFE? IS THAT THE 'FULLNESS OF LIFE' THAT GOD CALLS ME TO?

Father God, grant me courage to step out of my comfort zone to explore the paths you have prepared for my life that I might take my place a s part of of mighty army bringing alive your Kingdom in a needy and broken world. Amen

THE ONLY REAL FAILURE IS FAILURE TO TRY

PASSION IN WORSHIP

56

Q. DOES MY DISCIPLESHIP WOBBLE WHEN I'M UNHAPPY AT HOW GOD SEEMS TO ACT IN THE LIVES OF THOSE AROUND ME?

4 Notes to Self
* Be diligent and consistent in your obedience to God.
* Don't mistake God's love for casual pally-ness.
* Anticipate blessing when God is in the house.
* You can't go overboard when worshipping the living God.

Father God, free me from self-consciousness to worship you with all my heart, just as David did, and not be tied by what others may think appropriate. Amen

DAVID *then took up residence in the fortress and called it the City of David. He built up the area around it, from the terraces inward. And he became more and more powerful, because the Lord God Almighty was with him. Now Hiram king of Tyre sent envoys to David, along with cedar logs and carpenters and stonemasons, and they built a palace for David. Then David knew that the Lord had established him as king over Israel and had exalted his kingdom for the sake of his people Israel. 2 Samuel 5:6-7,9-12*

After yet more fighting against the Philistines - they must have been sick of the sight of each other by now - where David inquires of God how to approach the battle, obeys and wins, it is then time to bring the Ark of the Covenant to Jerusalem.

At first sight, what follows seems vindictively unnecessary. As the cart carrying the Ark wobbles on the road, Uzzah, apparently innocently, puts his hand out to steady it. But: ... *The Lord's anger burned against Uzzah because of his irreverent act; therefore God struck him down, and he died there beside the ark of God. 2 Samuel 6:7*
David is furious at this, and sulks: *He was not willing to take the ark of the Lord to be with him in the City of David. Instead, he took it to the house of Obed-Edom the Gittite. The ark of the Lord remained in the house of Obed-Edom the Gittite for three months, and the Lord blessed him and his entire household. 2 Samuel 6:10-11*

When David hears about this, he puts an end to his sulking and, now taking note of God's historic instructions for carrying the Ark, it is brought, without incident, into Jerusalem with much dancing and rejoicing: *Wearing a linen ephod, David was dancing before the Lord with all his might. 2 Samuel 6:14*

DAVID WAS DANCING BEFORE THE LORD WITH ALL HIS MIGHT

ADULTERY

DAVID

57

A time of peace follows and David wants to build a temple for the Ark to replace the moveable tent it has been kept in. Nice thought, but not God's plan. It is to be his son who will build it.

But God promises that, just as He has been with David so far, He will establish what was to become the Line of David that would, of course, lead to none other than Jesus Christ. David finds it amazing that God wants to use him, but accepts it and responds in worship. *Lord, you are God! Your covenant is trustworthy, and you have promised these good things to your servant. 2 Samuel 7:28*

Soon, though, its back to war and God gives David victory wherever he goes. We also read that: *David reigned over all Israel, doing what was just and right for all his people. 2 Samuel 8:15*

All of which, makes what follows quite startling. Whilst his army is out on the battlefield, David is lounging around on his balcony, ogling at the glamorous woman next door, which leads to adultery and then the organised killing of her husband, when it becomes apparent that she is pregnant and the king wants to cover up his actions. How on earth could this have happened? The saying goes "the devil makes work for idle hands" and Proverbs 21:25 points out that: *The craving of a sluggard will be the death of him, because his hands refuse to work.*

The reasons behind the chain of events are not difficult to work out. David's idleness led to wandering eyes and his acceptance of the prevailing culture of polygamy opened the door to his adultery. Solving everything with the sword gave a way out of his misdemeanour, with his absolute power as monarch leading him to think that he could get away with it.

> Q. AM I ALERT TO THE DANGERS OF IDLENESS AND WANDERING EYES?

> Father God, remind me to put on, at all times, the 'full armour of God' *(Ephesians 6)* and not rely on my own strength to live a pure and holy life that is pleasing to You and glorifies Your name. Amen

> ... ALL OF WHICH, MAKES WHAT FOLLOWS QUITE STARTLING

TACKLING TEMPTATION

58

Q. DO I HAVE PEOPLE IN PLACE TO HOLD ME ACCOUNTABLE FOR MY ACTIONS?

Father God, open my eyes to any dangers that might be present in my lifestyle and any weaknesses in my character that the devil can exploit ... and stir me to take appropriate action to avoid them. Amen

MAKING THE LINK BETWEEN THAT WHICH IS SWEET AND TEMPTING TO ITS DEADLY CONSEQUENCES IS CRUCIAL

BUT David couldn't get away with it, as God is on the case and confronts David through the prophet, Nathan. But not for nine months, as we learn that Bathsheba had moved in, become David's wife and given birth to a son in the interim.

God's judgment, when it comes, is proportionate to David's sin: *"This is what the Lord says: 'Out of your own household I am going to bring calamity on you. Before your very eyes I will take your wives and give them to one who is close to you, and he will sleep with your wives in broad daylight. You did it in secret, but I will do this thing in broad daylight before all Israel.'" Then David said to Nathan, "I have sinned against the Lord." Nathan replied, "The Lord has taken away your sin. You are not going to die. But because by doing this you have shown utter contempt for the Lord, the son born to you will die." 2 Samuel 12:11-14*

What can we take from this sorry affair? The apostle Peter summed it up pretty well: *Be alert and of sober mind. Your enemy the devil prowls around like a roaring lion looking for someone to devour. Resist him, standing firm in the faith, because you know that the family of believers throughout the world is undergoing the same kind of sufferings. 1 Peter 5:8-9*

But the battle can be joined before temptation stands in front of us, as Paul tells us: *Do not conform to the pattern of this world, but be transformed by the renewing of your mind. Then you will be able to test and approve what God's will is - his good, pleasing and perfect will. Romans 12:2*

David had left himself vulnerable to attack through his life choices and then, ironically in light of his early experience as a shepherd, couldn't hold back the lion when it pounced. Making the link between that which is sweet and tempting to its deadly consequences is crucial.

THE COST OF SIN

59

Q. DO I RECOGNISE AND CONFRONT MY INNATE SINFULNESS ... OR DO I TRY AND EXCUSE IT?

> Father God, open my eyes to see the needs of those around me who are struggling with the consequences of their own actions. Grant me love and compassion towards them, not a judgmental attitude and help me to enable them to get back on their feet. Amen

AS GOD'S MAN ON THE SPOT, IT WAS HIM AND HIS NAME THAT I HAD LET DOWN

IN case we tut-tut, however, but by the grace of God, there would go all of us. Although David has to face immediate pain and a lifetime of difficulty as a result of his sin, he comes clean with God (Psalm 51 giving us an insight to his response), is forgiven and resumes his life.

What this incident flags up is that forgiveness isn't a magic wand to eliminate all evidence and consequence of sin. Sin is more than a technical breach of regulations. It impacts the very fabric of life and relationships and is a costly affair. It immediately cost the life of David's son. Ultimately of course, it cost the life of another Son of David, sacrificed for us on a cross.

As referred to previously, I was going through a very difficult period at work as I wrote this. Looking back, I guess the progression of the situation was classic.

Disbelief at what is found; denial that its as bad as it becomes apparent it is; distress at the pressures it brings; despair that it will ever be solved; depression as exhaustion sets in whilst trying to remedy things. It was at this point that I cried out to my friends who swiftly gathered round to support and pray for me. All through, daily Bible readings had seemed strangely relevant to where I found myself.

As I wrote these paragraphs on David, it helped me to see that, although I felt very much let down by others and the tendency is always to want to point the finger of blame, actually I was the director of the project that went wrong, and ultimately it came down to my lack of diligence in oversight that let things get to where they had. And here comes the crunch. As God's man on the spot, it was Him and His name that I had let down.

FORGIVENESS

DAVID

60

DAVID saw that he had let God down in his situation with Bathsheba: *Against you, you only, have I sinned and done what is evil in your sight; so you are right in your verdict and justified when you judge. Psalm 51:4*

In my situation, as mentioned above, I had sought to claim one of my favourite Bible verses: *Do not be anxious about anything, but in every situation, by prayer and petition, with thanksgiving, present your requests to God. And the peace of God, which transcends all understanding, will guard your hearts and your minds in Christ Jesus. Philippians 4:6-7*

But this was not getting to the heart of the matter. Things still needed resolving as I pressed forward, but my hope was that, having come to recognise God's perspective on what had happened, I could again start to know His peace and joy. Forgiveness is indeed costly. But it is also real.

Look what comes next in the story. *Then David comforted his wife Bathsheba, and he went to her and made love to her. She gave birth to a son, and they named him Solomon. The Lord loved him. Samuel 12:24*

God doesn't go all coy with David. The relationship is restored and God loved David's new son, Solomon and blessed him. However, the remainder of David's life is plagued by family tensions, deceit and in-fighting.

First off, sons of David's different wives vie for the upper hand in love, and before long Absalom has his sights on his father's throne.

For a man anointed as king, promised an everlasting dynasty, and with a track record as a fearless and valiant warrior, David's response seems out of character: *Then David said to all his officials who were with him in Jerusalem, "Come! We must flee, or none of us will escape from Absalom. We must leave immediately, or he will move quickly to overtake us and bring ruin on us and put the city to the sword." 2 Samuel 15:14*

Q. HOW EASILY DO I ACCEPT FORGIVENESS AND ALLOW MYSELF TO MOVE ON?

Father God, give me a bigger vision of Your forgiveness - that I might fully grasp the completeness of Your unmerited grace. Forgive me for clinging onto the idea that I can do some thing myself to warrant Your pardon - for You have done it all. Amen

AGAINST YOU, YOU ONLY HAVE I SINNED AND DONE WHAT IS EVIL IN YOUR SIGHT

UPSTART SON

61

Q. WHAT CAN I DO TO HELP BUILD STRONG RELATIONSHIPS WITHIN MY BROADER FAMILY?

He reached down from on high and took hold of me; He drew me out of deep waters. He rescued me from my powerful enemy, from my foes, who were too strong for me. They confronted me in the day of my disaster, but the Lord was my support.
2 Samuel 22:17-19

Father God, enable me to see the potential impact for the future of actions I take and words I speak today. Grant me a disciplined tongue and wisdom to react generously to differences of opinion with those nearest to me. Amen

HAVING spent years as the anointed king-in-waiting running away from the king he would replace, now as king we find David on the run from his own son, who wants to be king himself. If you made it up, no-one would believe you!

Absalom enters a Jerusalem abandoned by its king and sleeps with David's deserted concubines on the palace roof "in the sight of all Israel", thus fulfilling God's word to David through Nathan.

In a soap opera, this stuff would be pretty unpalatable. It is even harder to stomach in the world of God and His anointed leader.

It all goes positively déjà-vu, as we see David's men eventually joining battle with his upstart son, who gets stuck in the branches of a tree and is run though by David's commander in chief. David, as with his previous arch adversary, Saul, is distraught at the news of his son's death. David returns to Jerusalem unsure of whether he's going to be accepted or not, and arrives back to encounter opposing factions wrestling for position and power.

Unsurprisingly, an unsuccessful coup follows and the remaining years of David's life follow a now familiar pattern of crisis (getting to grips with a 3 year famine) and conflict (you guessed it, with his old friends, the Philistines).

We learn that David saw off an attempt by another of his sons, Adonijah, to take the throne and successfully establish Solomon before he rested with his ancestors and was buried in the City of David. (1 Kings 2:10). Prior to that though, in 2 Samuel 22 17-19 (see side panel), we are treated to a final insight into what made David tick, as he pours out his heart to God in words that were to become known as Psalm 18.

RIGHTEOUSNESS?

DAVID

62

THAT David knew complete forgiveness by God seems fine ... great, actually. But my eyebrows rise considerably as David then goes on: *The Lord has dealt with me according to my righteousness; according to the cleanness of my hands he has rewarded me. For I have kept the ways of the Lord; I am not guilty of turning from my God. All his laws are before me; I have not turned away from his decrees. I have been blameless before him and have kept myself from sin. The Lord has rewarded me according to my righteousness, according to my cleanness in his sight.*
2 Samuel 22:21-25

How can an adulterer and murderer claim he has clean hands, been blameless and kept himself from sin? David is not looking through worldly eyes here. The prism through which he views his life and his God anticipate the confidence expressed by the apostle John a millennium later:

If we claim to be without sin, we deceive ourselves and the truth is not in us. If we confess our sins, he is faithful and just and will forgive us our sins and purify us from all unrighteousness. 1 John 1:8-9

So when David says he has kept the ways of the Lord and is not guilty of turning from his God, he is embracing an understanding that equates righteousness not with living a fault free life (only one person ever did that, and it clearly wasn't David!); rather, one that accepts we will get it wrong, but brings faults openly before God in the certainty that we will be forgiven.

This is the sure hope of the Christian gospel ... 1,000 years before its time.

Q. HAVE I REALLY GRASPED WHAT CHRIST HAS DONE FOR ME ON THE CROSS?

Father God, open my eyes afresh to the favour that you have bestowed on me - your righteousness for my sinfulness. Amazing grace indeed. Thank you. Amen

THIS IS THE SURE HOPE OF THE CHRISTIAN GOSPEL .... 1,000 YEARS BEFORE ITS TIME

THE LORD HAS REWARDED ME ACCORDING TO MY RIGHTEOUSNESS ACCORDING TO MY CLEANNESS IN HIS SIGHT

FINAL WORDS

63

DAVID'S final words, whilst having a weary and reflective feel to them, are spoken with a considered confidence:

The God of Israel spoke, the Rock of Israel said to me: 'When one rules over people in righteousness, when he rules in the fear of God, he is like the light of morning at sunrise on a cloudless morning, like the brightness after rain that brings grass from the earth.' "If my house were not right with God, surely he would not have made with me an everlasting covenant, arranged and secured in every part; surely he would not bring to fruition my salvation and grant me my every desire. 2 Samuel 23:3-5

In spite of having to battle through a frankly exhausting life, David had run the race set before him and crossed the finishing line secure in the knowledge that his salvation had been brought to fruition.

You can't ask for more than that. Bravo David.

Q. HOW MIGHT I SUMMARISE MY LIFE TO DATE?

Father God, remind me daily of the calling you have placed on my life, so I may pursue it steadfastly through thick and thin, and run the race you have set before me with all my heart, soul and strength. Amen

WHEN ONE RULES OVER PEOPLE IN RIGHTEOUSNESS ... HE IS LIKE THE LIGHT OF MORNING AT SUNRISE

PRAYING with DAVID

Have mercy on me, O God
according to Your great love.
According to Your great compassion
blot out my transgressions.
Cleanse me with hyssop and I will be clean;
wash me and I will be whiter than snow.
Create in me a pure heart, O God
and renew a steadfast spirit within me.
Restore to me the joy of Your salvation
and grant me a willing spirit to sustain me.
Open my lips, Lord
and my mouth will declare Your praise.
Amen

ACCORDING TO YOUR GREAT COMPASSION
BLOT OUT MY TRANSGRESSIONS
Psalm 51

CANAANITE WOMAN
Matthew 15

JESUS   #7

64

A Canaanite woman asks Jesus to heal her daughter. He at first seems to resist, as she's not a Jew. But the woman persists with a humorous analogy of dog's picking up crumbs from beneath the family table. See Matthew 15

Q. HOW CLOSELY DO I ENGAGE WITH GOD IN PRAYER?

This encounter speaks persuasively of Jesus' humanity and his pleasure in engaging with people, whether or not they currently profess faith in Him.

Jesus' conclusion? *"Woman, you have great faith! Your request is granted." And her daughter was healed at that moment.* Matthew 15:22

Lord Jesus, draw me to spend more time with you. Send me to spend more time with others. Amen

WE ARE GOD'S WORKMANSHIP, CREATED IN CHRIST JESUS TO DO GOOD WORKS, WHICH GOD PREPARED IN ADVANCE FOR US TO DO. *Ephesians 2:10*